the
ENNEAGRAM
for **Relationships**

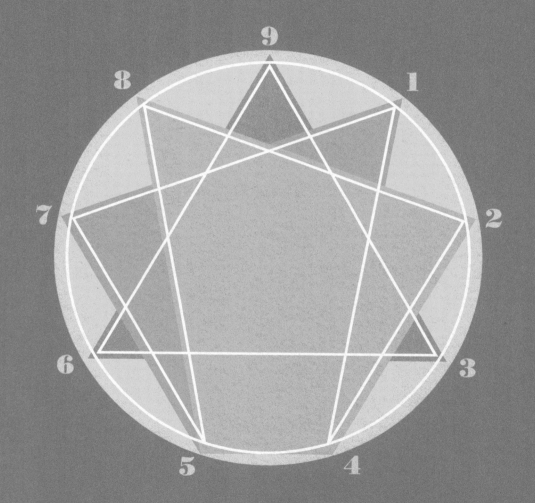

the
ENNEAGRAM
for Relationships

Transform Your Connections with Friends, Family, Colleagues, and in Love

Ashton Whitmoyer-Ober, MA

ROCKRIDGE
PRESS

For general information on our other products and services or to obtain technical support, please contact our Customer Care Department within the United States at (866) 744-2665, or outside the United States at (510) 253-0500.

Rockridge Press publishes its books in a variety of electronic and print formats. Some content that appears in print may not be available in electronic books, and vice versa.

TRADEMARKS: Rockridge Press and the Rockridge Press logo are trademarks or registered trademarks of Callisto Media Inc. and/or its affiliates, in the United States and other countries, and may not be used without written permission. All other trademarks are the property of their respective owners. Rockridge Press is not associated with any product or vendor mentioned in this book.

Interior and Cover Designer: Stephanie Mautone
Art Producer: Sara Feinstein
Editor: Emily Angell
Production Editor: Emily Sheehan

Author photo courtesy of © Aubree Shannon Photography

ISBN: Print 978-1-64611-078-0 | eBook 978-1-64611-079-7
R0

This book is dedicated to all of the people out there who ever had someone tell them that they can't do something. You are my people. Keep on keeping on. Oh, and to my husband, Derek. You're the real MVP for keeping our house tidy and our dog fed during the writing of this book.

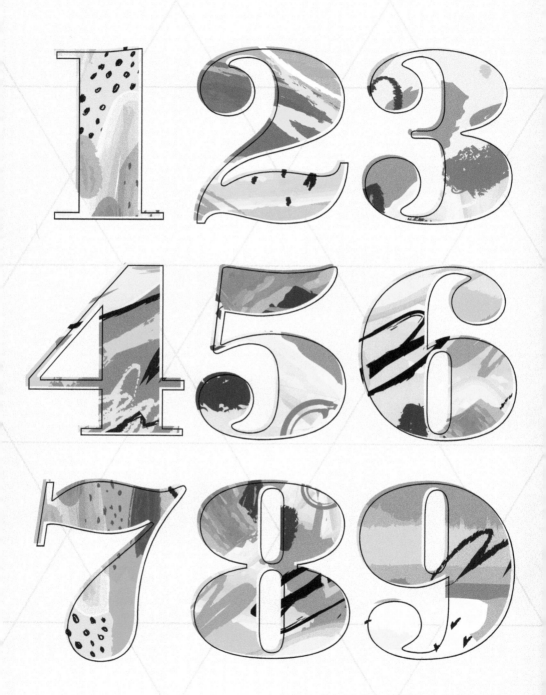

Contents

Introduction

Hi there. I'm Ashton, also known as Enneagram Ashton on Instagram. Thank you for joining me on this journey to learning and growing our relationships through the Enneagram. I've always been interested in personality tests. I remember asking my mom to take me to Barnes & Noble as a kid so I could browse the psychology section and pick out personality tests. That curiosity led me to later earn my bachelor's degree in psychology and my master's degree in community psychology and social change. I guess you could say that I've always been interested in how people and communities can strengthen, grow, and relate to one another, which led me to the Enneagram.

Before I became trained on the Enneagram, I kept hearing people talk about it: "It's similar to Myers–Briggs," and "it's a personality test." But I learned right away that it isn't actually a personality test. Myers–Briggs tells us who we are; the Enneagram tells us the motivations behind what we do. Three people at a social event could all be in a corner avoiding eye contact, but their motivations for standing in the corner could all be different. I decided that I absolutely needed to become an Enneagram coach, so I sought training and studied with Beth McCord of YourEnneagramCoach.com. I created an Instagram account to share my journey, and it turns out that a lot of people wanted to follow along. Most important, I have learned so much about myself and how I interact with colleagues, friends, romantic partners, family members, and even random people I pass on the street.

Author and Enneagram master teacher Ian Morgan Cron said, "The Enneagram doesn't put you in a box. It shows you the box you're already in and how to get out of it." The Enneagram is more than just a typing tool; it's a way to experience self-growth and understanding. Once I learned that I was a Two (The Helper), everything around me clicked—my personal and professional relationships, how I react in certain situations, why I made certain decisions. It also wasn't just important for me to identify these motivations for my own development; I was able to better communicate to others how to best interact with me as a Two and how to love and support me. I want you to experience that as well.

This book is a tool for you to strengthen the ways in which you interact with other people. It will teach you new ways to understand how you can be in healthy relationships with each Enneagram type. We will start with background information and the historical roots of the Enneagram. Then, prepare yourself to receive a wealth of information as we dive deep into each Enneagram type. Specifically, I'll be covering work relationships, friendships, romantic relationships, and familial relationships. Of course, there will also be background information on the strengths and weaknesses, childhood tendencies, and other characteristics of each of the nine types to give you a better understanding of the motivations behind each one.

Although the Enneagram can be an informative way to explore your personality and how you function with the people in your life, neither it nor this book is a crystal ball or a cure-all. I fully believe that understanding the Enneagram can help strengthen our relationships. However, if you are experiencing chronic stress, feeling down, or are involved in a stressful, unfulfilling, abusive, or unhealthy relationship, there are resources that can help you. There is no shame in asking for support, and I encourage you to seek out professional help.

I'm sure that you're tempted to skip ahead and read the chapter that relates to your type or maybe your partner's Enneagram type. But resist the urge, friends! We interact with many different people every day, and it is so important to read the entire book so you can learn how to best interact with everyone around you. The goal of this book is to help you understand the Enneagram, but it's so much more than that. By reading through the text, you are on a path to understanding the Enneagram and learning how to navigate your life and relationships. By learning how you and your loved ones interact in these partnerships, you are setting yourself up to have healthy and fulfilling relationships with everyone you meet.

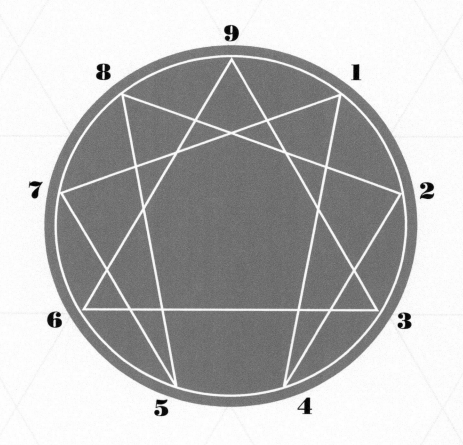

CHAPTER ONE

An Introduction to the Enneagram

Everyone has different levels of knowledge when it comes to the Enneagram and how to best use it in their lives. Before we dive into exploring the various relationships between the types, we first need to establish some foundational information about the Enneagram. In short, the Enneagram is an ancient typing system that goes beyond just explaining someone's personality. It takes into account why and how people think, react, and behave. But it doesn't just stop there. The Enneagram can also provide transformative growth for those who are ready to live up to the potential that life has to offer them.

What Is the Enneagram?

The conception of the Enneagram is difficult to pinpoint because it dates back thousands of years. This is what we do know: The Enneagram is rooted in psychology, spirituality, and self-observation, and has Asian and Middle Eastern roots dating back 2,000 to 4,000 years. In our modern world, the Enneagram is a model of the human psyche dividing people into nine different "types" and going deeper than traditional personality tests to discover motivations and not just tendencies.

What the Enneagram Isn't

There are also several misconceptions about the Enneagram. It does a disservice to the Enneagram to group it with personality tests such as the Myers–Briggs Type Indicator (MBTI) and StrengthsFinder 2.0. Although I am a huge believer in personality tests to identify who we are, I trained in the Enneagram because it goes far beyond a simple personality test. Traditional personality tests describe who we are, whereas the Enneagram explores the why and how and the motivations behind what we do. Additionally, traditional personality tests typically leave us wanting more. Self-reflection with the Enneagram gives us the opportunity to grow through behaviors and experiences using the Enneagram as a tool. After all, that's really what the Enneagram is: a tool to learn more about ourselves and our individual motivations and tendencies so we can grow into the best versions of ourselves.

A Brief History

Even though the Enneagram has been around for thousands of years, it has ebbed and flowed in popularity. Because the Enneagram wasn't introduced to the United States until researchers brought it here in the 1960s, according to The Enneagram Institute, it took time for people to learn about and understand this typing system. As with most things, I'm sure there were also skeptics. However, psychologists persisted, and it became more popular in the 1980s. Its real popularity didn't come about until the past 10 years, largely thanks to technology. Think about how much technology has advanced since the Enneagram was first introduced in the United States. Now we have cellphones, the Internet, social media, and search engines that people use to discover and learn more about the Enneagram. We have this information at our disposal, and people can post about it on social media and share it easily. The information propagated quickly and pretty soon, everyone was trying to determine their Enneagram type.

The Christian and Sufism Perspective

The Enneagram Institute said that some experts can trace the Enneagram back to Sufism, whereas others identify a clear connection to Christianity, specifically related to the seven deadly sins. It's clear that the Enneagram was rooted in religion, and many people used it to incorporate different faiths and religions into their daily practice.

The Modern-Day Enneagram

Even though the Enneagram originates from religion, it is now widely used in the secular world as part of a path toward self-actualization. Despite a confusing and somewhat complicated start, the rediscovery of the Enneagram in the 20th century is much clearer. George Gurdjieff, originally from Russia, was first introduced to the Enneagram while he was traveling in Afghanistan in the 1920s, according to Integrative 9, an Enneagram solutions company. He compared the Enneagram to a dance because of the movement within the model and even referred to himself as a "dance teacher." During the 1960s, Óscar Ichazo, who is credited with putting the modern Enneagram system together, according to The Enneagram In Business, was teaching the Enneagram at his Arica School in South America, which he founded as a place to teach his methods. Claudio Naranjo, an American psychiatrist who trained with Ichazo in Chile, first brought it back to the United States.

Prominent Figures in Enneagram History

Don Richard Riso and Russ Hudson, two of the most well-known Enneagram teachers and authors, were some of the first notable Enneagram researchers in the United States after they were introduced to the Enneagram in 1975. After publishing several books based on their research, they created and opened The Enneagram Institute in 1997 in New York City. Together, they developed the Riso–Hudson Enneagram Type Indicator, commonly known as the RHETI, one of the most popular and accurate Enneagram tests. Other popular Enneagram teachers, authors, and experts include Beatrice Chestnut, Ginger Lapid-Bogda, Beth McCord, David Daniels, and Jerry Wagner. Many Enneagram teachers and authors share their own Enneagram types as a way to further connect with their readers. I encourage you to explore writings from those who share an Enneagram type with you. There is something oddly comforting about listening to others speak in a way that makes sense to your being.

The Structure of the Enneagram

The word Enneagram is derived from the Greek words *ennea*, meaning "nine," and *gram*, meaning "what is written or drawn." The Enneagram is made up of nine personality types that are located on different points of a symbol. Though the figure seems complicated at first, all of the various shapes work together to create the Enneagram.

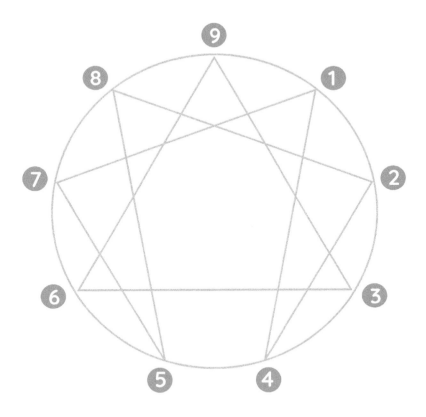

The Enneagram Figure

Sometimes it's easier for people to understand the way that the Enneagram functions if they draw it themselves. The Enneagram symbol is made up of three parts: an outer circle, a triangle, and a hexad. The circle represents the oneness of life, and the triangle represents that the symbol has three separate sources. Some Enneagram experts teach this differently, but I view these sources as the "triads": the *fear triad*, *anger triad*, and *shame triad*. We will talk more about those later in this chapter. The third shape in the Enneagram symbol is the hexad, a six-pointed figure, which represents the way we all move through life, and within this hexad are more sets of triangles. These arrows, or lines, are sometimes referred to as integration/disintegration arrows or stress/growth arrows. They show us where each type goes when they are experiencing stress and growth. The combination of all three shapes, lines, and the nine numbers creates what we know as the powerful structure of the Enneagram.

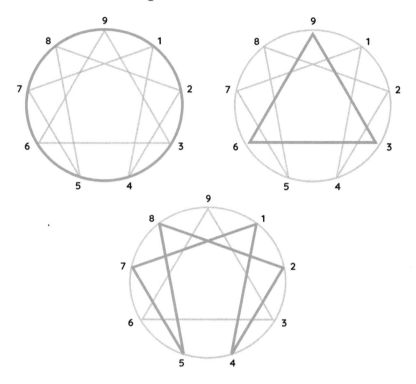

Centers of Intelligence

The Enneagram is divided into three sections, with three types in each section. We call these sections "centers" because they are always at the center of our biggest assets and greatest liabilities. Types Eight, Nine, and One are in the *instinctive center,* meaning that the best and worst things about their personality types are due to their instinctual drives. Types Two, Three, and Four are in the *feeling center,* which means that the best and worst things about their types are related to feelings. Finally, Types Five, Six, and Seven are in the *thinking center,* which—you may have guessed it—means that the best and worst things about their types are based on their thought processes and thinking patterns. These centers are also associated with different emotions. Those who are in the instinctive center typically struggle with anger: Each type just might display it differently. People who are in the feeling center are more likely to suffer from shame. Finally, those who are in the thinking center usually identify as struggling with fear.

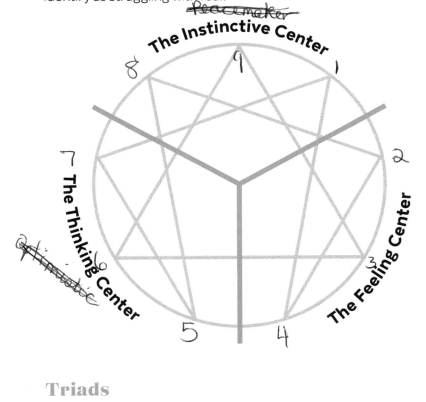

Triads

The Enneagram types can also be grouped together as harmony triads, or groups of three. The three triads are the *optimistic triad,* the *competency triad,* and the *intensity triad,* because the Enneagram types in the triads all have these traits in common. The optimistic triad contains types Seven (The Enthusiast), Nine (The Peacemaker), and Two (The Helper). These types view life in a positive way and are the most optimistic types on the

Enneagram. Type Seven is the topmost optimistic number on the Enneagram. The competency triad contains Types One (The Reformer), Three (The Achiever), and Five (The Investigator). The types within this triad value being competent, as well as being seen as competent by others. Specifically, for Type Ones, competency means being right, whereas for Threes it means knowing how to achieve the success they desire. For Fives, competency is equivalent to a deep understanding. The intensity triad is a combination of Types Four (The Individualist), Six (The Loyalist), and Eight (The Challenger). The types in this triad are the most intense on the Enneagram, but each type demonstrates their intensity differently. For example, Type Four has more of an emotional intensity, whereas Type Six's intensity stems from a worried, doubt-filled mind. Type Eight's intensity is felt by others when they are in the presence of them.

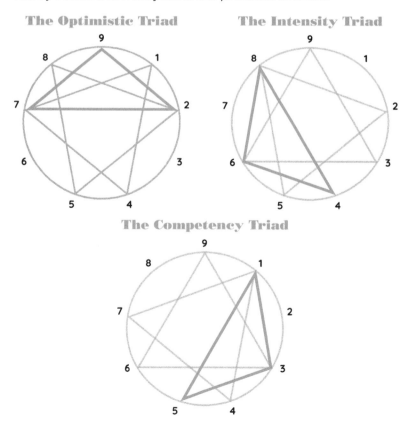

The Optimistic Triad

The Intensity Triad

The Competency Triad

Wings

Another factor that can affect an individual's Enneagram type are what we call "wings." Wings are the numbers directly on either side of your main Enneagram number. This allows for characteristics of the wings to play a part in your overall personality type. For example, an Enneagram One (The Reformer) can pull qualities from an Enneagram Nine (The Peacemaker) and/or an Enneagram Two (The Helper). Many people assume that your wing is just the type that had the second highest number when you took a test or the type that resonates with you the most after your main type. Neither assumption is true, as the wings absolutely must be on either side of your type—you know, like wings. Another common misconception is that you absolutely must have a wing. The reality is that some people don't feel like they utilize their wings, and that's fine and totally normal. Some people also might feel like they rely on one wing more than another. It really depends on the person and the motivations behind their behaviors. Sometimes, part of the self-development work of the Enneagram is learning how to incorporate the healthy qualities of your wings into your everyday life. Usually people have a more dominant wing, but being able to utilize healthy qualities of both wings allows for substantial personal growth within your Enneagram type.

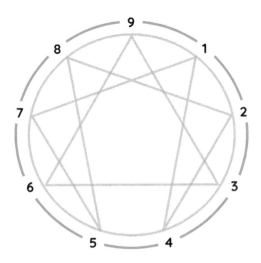

The Nine Types

Experts use a variety of names for the nine Enneagram types. Throughout this book, I will use the names created by authors and Enneagram experts Riso and Hudson. Type One is known as *The Reformer*. They are structured, practical, and balanced. They are motivated by a desire to be good, and they see things in black and white. Type Two is *The Helper*. They are extremely giving of their time, energy, and resources. They are motivated by a need to be wanted and loved. Type Three is called *The Achiever* because of their strong need to accomplish things in life. They are goal-oriented, hardworking, and often competitive. They are motivated by a desire to be seen as valuable. Type Four is referred to as *The Individualist*. They are often artistic, emotional, and creative. They are motivated by a need to be seen as unique and unlike anyone else. Type Five is known as *The Investigator*. They are intellectual, withdrawn, and independent. They are motivated by a strong need to be seen as competent to those around them. Type Six is *The Loyalist*. They are committed, responsible, and anxious. These individuals are motivated by a need to feel secure in their relationships and environment. Type Seven is referred to as *The Enthusiast* because of their ability to radiate optimism. They are spontaneous and scattered and seek adventure in all that they do. These individuals are motivated by a need to feel satisfied and content and often have the biggest fear of missing out. Type Eight is known as *The Challenger*. They are strong, assertive, and resourceful. They are motivated by a desire to protect themselves and not be seen as weak or vulnerable. Type Nine is referred to as *The Peacemaker*. They are calm, conflict-averse, and open-minded. They are motivated by a desire to maintain peace and wholeness in whatever they do.

Why Are There Nine Types?

The nine types are nine personalities and nine ways of thinking and behaving. But why nine? The three core numbers for each triad (Three, Six, and Nine) form the triangle within the Enneagram figure. With those numbers as the core points, each has an inner and outer focus. The feeling center/shame triad has Type Three as the core point, Type Two as the outer focus, and Type Four as the inner focus. The thinking center/fear triad has Type Six as the core point, Type Five as the outer focus, and Type Seven as the inner focus. Finally, the instinctive center/anger triad has Type Nine as the core point, Type Eight as the outer focus, and Type One as the inner focus. With each triad having a core point, outer focus, and inner focus, the diagram is made up of nine types total. And that is the Enneagram.

What Does All of This Tell Us about Ourselves?

As we discussed, although personality tests are great at telling us who we are, the Enneagram focuses on why and how we do the things we do. It reveals our deepest, and sometimes most unknown, secrets about ourselves and our desires, motivations, and fears. Ultimately, the Enneagram is a tool to promote self-awareness and personal development. We can use the Enneagram as a way to learn more about ourselves and the people around us. The Enneagram can enlighten us on how we work with others, how we interact in relationships and friendships, and who we are within our family unit.

Compatibility

Although some Enneagram types may be more compatible than others, anyone can be compatible with anyone else if they are living within a healthy state of their type. On the opposite side of that, any type can be incompatible if they are considered to be on the unhealthy side of their type. Some Enneagram type couplings are more common than others, but there are never types that are more compatible than others. I encourage you to strive to be the best version of yourself before trying to determine your compatibility with others.

If You Don't Already Know Your Type . . .

This book doesn't offer a test for you to figure out your Enneagram type. And I would even say that taking a test isn't the best way to discover which Enneagram type resonates the most with you. My recommendation is to take a test to start, but don't end there. Spend time reflecting on your biggest fears and desires to see if any of them resonate with the different Enneagram types. I also recommend reviewing the results of the test with someone who has been trained as an Enneagram coach or expert, like myself and others in the large Enneagram coaching network. The Enneagram test I recommend is the Riso–Hudson Enneagram Type Indicator (RHETI). I also recommend Beth McCord's free test at YourEnneagramCoach.com for a faith-based perspective to the Enneagram.

The Biggest Temptation

It's also important that you never try to type someone yourself. Although it might seem obvious to you that someone is a certain Enneagram type, you don't always know their motivations behind what they do or how they act. You might know that one of your friends is very assertive and assume that they are an Enneagram Eight. However, the motivation for their assertiveness may be that they want to be seen as valuable (Three) versus that they don't want to be seen as weak (Eight). It's also important that you never try to type a child or say that they're acting like a certain Enneagram type. They need to figure out their type on their own, otherwise they may try to act like a certain type for approval. We also don't want to put people in a "box" and predict certain behaviors based on the types we assume they are. As I go through the individual types, I note some famous people of each type, which may seem contradictory to what I'm telling you here. However, the major difference is that I am trained in the Enneagram and can better speculate on someone's type based on their actions, things they have said, and how they present themselves in public.

Grow into Your Best Self

The Enneagram is an astounding way to grow into living your best life by being authentically you. Even more amazing is the way that the Enneagram transforms relationships with colleagues, friends, life partners, and family members. You'll learn more about how the Enneagram can help you and your relationships in the chapters ahead.

Type

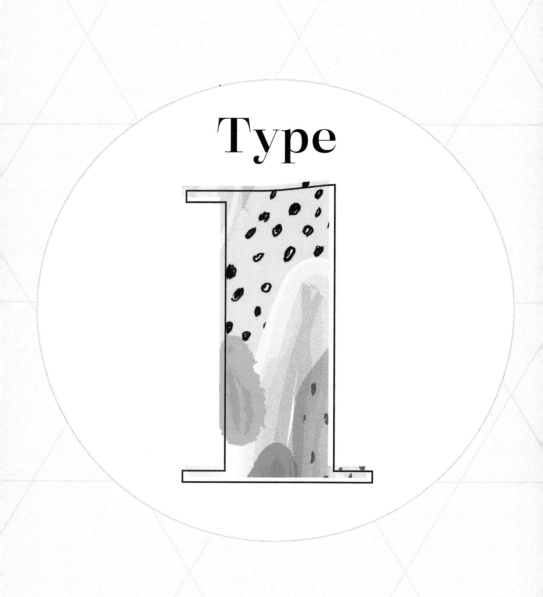

CHAPTER TWO

The Reformer

E nneagram One is *The Reformer,* although this type is also known as *The Perfectionist* among some Enneagram experts. Reformers are concerned with knowing right from wrong and having structure in their world. It's important to remember that structure can mean different things to different people. Their personality is based on whatever is "right" to them. Their biggest fear is being corrupt or "bad," and their biggest desire is to be good and have integrity. Reformers have many great qualities, such as efficiency, productivity, honesty, orderliness, practicality, and a strong work ethic. However, there are some negative qualities that could creep in if Ones are going through a hard time or living in a state of stress. For example, Ones can be judgmental, obsessive, critical of others and themselves, controlling, and high strung. It's important to understand all of the qualities of an Enneagram One as we discuss various types of relationships that one can have with them. Pun definitely intended.

Getting to Know The Reformer

A Reformer is a person who makes changes to something in order to improve it. I can totally see why Riso and Hudson picked this word to describe the Enneagram One. Ones are definitely the people who will try to improve everything around them. This includes themselves, other people, their environment, and their relationships. Sometimes this "improving" can get them into trouble when people didn't ask for their help in the first place. It can also affect others negatively when Ones start judging those around them because their lives look different from their own.

Here are some other character traits of a One:

» Principled

» Perfectionist

» Impatient

» Wise

» Realistic

» Competent

» Rule-follower

» Ambitious

» Practical

» Independent

Common Mistypes

Some people may think that they are an Enneagram One if they tend to be more organized and concerned about following rules. However, many people enjoy following rules (at least I hope) but aren't necessarily Ones. People also tend to think they are Ones because they are extreme planners. Although these stereotypes do fit an Enneagram One, they are not the only types who have these characteristics. Some common mistypes for an Enneagram One are Enneagram Six, Eight, and Three. Types One and Six seem similar because they are both extremely loyal and both experience worry at times. However, one key difference is that Sixes aren't big risk-takers, whereas Ones are willing to take risks to make the world a better place. Similarly, Ones and Eights are often mistyped because they both feel like it's up to them to create change in the world. Eights struggle with vulnerability, whereas Ones are quick to be vulnerable with those who are closest to them. Ones and Threes are similar because they are both driven by achievement. The biggest difference is that Threes are more concerned about image, whereas Ones are mostly concerned with simply doing what is right.

Childhood

When exploring the way different people interact, it can sometimes be helpful to look back on who they were and how they behaved as a child. Reformers as children can often be identified by the amount of time they spend criticizing themselves if they aren't perfect. They try to achieve perfection in projects, presentations, academics, sports, and anything else they are involved in. They are often seen as competitive; however, most people wouldn't know that Ones are mostly competing with themselves. Enneagram One children definitely feel like they have a hard time living up to the expectations of those in their lives, such as parents, caretakers, and even friends. It may be hard for them to finish projects because they are just not "perfect" enough. Many times, Reformers take on the role of "parent" in their friend group or with their younger siblings. As kids, they are extreme rule-followers and keep everyone else in line. If Ones break any rules, they will feel guilty or mad at themselves because they might no longer be perceived as "good."

Worldview

The Reformers view the world as if it's flawed. This goes for their own world, their friends' worlds, their family's world, and the entire planet, too. They look at the world as being imperfect, and therefore, they have to do whatever they can to perfect or fix the world around them. They consider it their mission to correct the flaws of the world, whether that be resolving injustices, trying to recycle more, or even just changing the toilet paper roll and putting it back on in the correct way (because everyone knows there actually is a correct way). The Reformer believes that the world is flawed, and it's their job to correct it.

Strengths and Weaknesses

Because Enneagram Ones have a critical voice playing in their heads constantly, they might think that they have more weaknesses than strengths. However, Ones have many strong qualities that make them loyal and dependable people. Because Ones need structure and discipline, they will create a plan and stick to it. They are great at accomplishing tasks, no matter how big or how small. Because Ones have a strong desire to be the best they can be, they will also bring out the best in everyone around them. However, strengths do not come without weaknesses. Because Ones want so badly to be perfect, they can sometimes be judgmental of others if they aren't as perfect as they feel they are. Depending on where they are on the healthy versus unhealthy scale, Ones can sometimes come off as being extremely critical and having unreasonably high expectations of those around them. This trait could come out as a One being displeased about someone's personality characteristics, or they could be critical about the way that someone folds a fitted sheet. (Let's be honest, does anyone really know how to fold a fitted sheet?) Because Enneagram Ones are within the anger triad, they can definitely exert that emotion when they feel their expectations aren't being met. If they don't outwardly express that anger, they can turn it inward and become depressed and withdrawn, much like the unhealthy qualities of an Enneagram Four. Another trait that could result in a trouble spot for The Reformer is the constant need to "do." This could be perceived as a strength or a weakness, but it is important for Ones to be aware of it so they can remind themselves the world won't end if they stop to breathe or put off mopping their floors for one day.

Dealing with Conflict

Enneagram Ones address conflict head-on in order to move on from it as quickly as possible. They have no problem telling you when you've done something that hurts their feelings.

THREE FAMOUS REFORMERS

You will recognize a famous One from the fact that they have a mission or purpose. A lot of famous Reformers are politicians with a specific platform, or actors who speak out about a certain cause.

- Julie Andrews is the epitome of an Enneagram One. She is a self-proclaimed perfectionist and considers herself to be principled and structured.

- Another famous Enneagram One is Kate Middleton, the Duchess of Cambridge. She is extremely passionate about charity work, specifically when it comes to causes that impact children.

- A famous Enneagram One character from film is Mary Poppins. She is a nanny who visits a dysfunctional family to make it right, to add structure to chaos. A true Reformer.

Enneagram One Wings

Not every Reformer is going to be the same. As I mentioned earlier, there are different traits that pertain to the personality, which could make two Enneagram Ones look entirely different. I always like to explain this by comparing Enneagram types to paint colors. For example, say that Type One is purple. People can be the same type but have entirely different personality traits, just as there are many varied and different shades of purple. An example of this is when the wings are involved. A Reformer who connects more strongly with their Two wing is going to be more giving and helpful. They will make sure that others' needs are being met. They also might struggle more with caring what other people think about them. A Reformer who accesses their Nine wing more will be focused on making sure that the environment remains peaceful. They might be more passive-aggressive and not let their anger show as easily. The Nine wing would also bring out a tendency to be a little less judgmental and a little more understanding. Again, the goal is to rely on both wings, but some people might lean more toward one or the other.

Relationships with The Reformer

When thinking about relationships with someone who is an Enneagram One, three words come to mind: order, dedication, and responsibility. If you're in any kind of relationship with an Enneagram One, prepare to be amazed at their ability to get things done in a way that seems seamless, while being fully dedicated to the relationship that you are in together. Ones bring many amazing qualities into relationships but may also exhibit traits that they need to overcome.

Let's go back to order, dedication, and responsibility. What I mean by order is not necessarily what we call being a "clean freak." Sure, many Ones do pride themselves in maintaining an organized space and environment; however, order extends beyond whether there are perfect vacuum lines on the carpet. Order, specifically in relationships, means that you will most likely never have to wonder where things are located. But it also means that your relationship with this person will be well-thought-out and structured. Enneagram Ones don't just begin relationships with people unless they have already thought it through.

This brings me to the next word: dedication. Because Ones are thoughtful in their decision-making, if they are in any type of relationship with you, they are 100 percent dedicated to that relationship. The best way I know how to explain this trait to you is to introduce you to my friend, Molly. Molly is a true Enneagram One. Truth and justice are very important to her, she's never been late a day in her life, and she views things as right or wrong, with no in-between. She is also, probably, the most dedicated friend I have ever known—and not just to me, but to everyone with whom she has a relationship. Her longevity in relationships displays how dedicated she is, but it extends well beyond the length of her relationships. Dedication in relationships for an Enneagram One means they will be dedicated to ensuring that everyone's needs are met, problems are resolved, and the relationship continues to grow.

Much like the other two, the topic of responsibility is a frequent determinant of an Enneagram One. They often feel responsible for their relationships and for the people in them. Because they desire truth and justice, Ones thrive in accepting the responsibility to demonstrate truth in their relationships. Ones are who you can call on to tell you if you look good in that outfit, whether you shouldn't go on that date, or what your next career move should be. They tend to be brutally honest in their opinions and assume that their opinions are facts.

Despite these incredible characteristics of Ones, they do have some trouble spots when it comes to relationships. Specifically, Ones can often be critical and judgmental when their friends or partners don't do things the way that they do. Most of the time, they don't even realize they are acting that way. They are so accustomed to feeling like they are being judged that sometimes they can't help but judge others. This could also lead to unmet expectations and resentment, which cause Ones to exhibit the negative characteristics of an Enneagram Four. Resentment is a fairly common thing that Ones experience, especially when they are unable to communicate how they are feeling. Effective communication between both partners is key to making things work with an Enneagram One.

Relationships with Colleagues

Relationships with coworkers are hard enough without the complication of differing personalities. Type Ones can be particularly difficult to work with because of their need for perfection. On the other hand, many people love to work with Ones because of their attention to detail, work ethic, and desire to follow the rules. Supervisors and managers especially love Enneagram Ones because they know Ones are reliable and hardworking. Colleagues of Ones may have conflicts with them if there is a power imbalance. What I mean is that Ones love to be in control. If they have a colleague who also wants to be in control, it can cause a significant amount of tension between them. People may also feel Ones are taking over when it comes to work projects and ideas. This is because Ones often feel they will be let down by the work someone else does, so they may as well just complete the task themselves. It's also important to think about how a type responds to stress because many work situations can be stressful. A One will shut down and withdraw as soon as they feel like they are entering a stressful situation. This could cause a breakdown in communication, and the problems may be left unresolved. Ultimately, resentment could become a key factor in an unhealthy work relationship.

I once met a woman named Susan who was an Enneagram One. She told me about a colleague that she had, Linda, who identified herself as an Enneagram Eight, The Challenger.

Dynamics between Ones and Eights can be tricky even outside of a work environment. Susan told me all about how bossy Linda was and that she always tried to take the lead on some projects they were supposed to be working on together. Susan had a hard time relinquishing control of those projects and felt that Linda wasn't doing her tasks the way that they should be completed. They ended up getting frustrated at each other and exchanged some harsh words.

There are a few things that were going on I was able to identify pretty quickly in this story. Reformers and Challengers have an interesting dynamic, and both like to be in charge and ultimately in control. In this situation, specifically, it was a work project and the two of them were trying to determine who the alpha was. Susan was also having a difficult time with Linda completing tasks differently than she was, which can be a typical trait of a Type One who is not living in a healthy state of growth. Additionally, both The Reformer and The Challenger are in the anger triad, meaning that their gut reaction is to respond to situations with anger. This could be the root of why they felt the need to react with harsh words. When working with others, it's important to be aware of how different Enneagram types respond so you can better anticipate situations and your own instinctive reactions.

Relationships with Friends

Reformers are some of the most loyal friends on the Enneagram. They are extremely reliable, dependable, and intentional with your time and your relationship with them. They are often the friend you can call when you need an honest opinion about that new guy you're seeing, the outfit you just bought that might be a little too tight, or how your new hair color really looks. Although they probably wouldn't have let you dye your hair that color in the first place, to be honest. This is because they see the world as black and white, with no in-between. Of course, they will be direct with you, because that's how everyone is supposed to be (according to them). They don't think they're being too direct or mean, because they feel it would be mean if they kept their mouth shut and said nothing at all. You want to be friends with a Reformer. They might get frustrated with you if you're constantly late. They might be annoyed at you if you try to break some rules. You may not always understand why they have to be so structured. But you will know and understand that you have a friend who is always in your corner.

I told you about my friend Molly, the most dedicated friend I've ever had, and a true Enneagram One. Molly is a great depiction of a healthy One, as she knows and understands that how I function as a Type Two is different from how she sees and interacts with the world. But it took us some work to get there, like any and all relationships. Molly and I met when we were in high school and became quick friends. She was older than most people in our grade, which meant that she was able to drive before the rest of us in our friend group. I'm sure this had some perks and downsides, as she always had to pick us up and drive us everywhere. I think she liked it that way, though, because she was the natural leader of our group—and not just because she was older than us, but because she was a rule-follower. She kept us in line, making sure we did our homework and excelled in school while still having a great time and creating memories. We all attended different colleges across different states but stayed connected. And I honestly think it was because of Molly. The leader of the group. The intentional friend. The glue that keeps people together. The Enneagram One.

Romantic Relationships

Reformers in romantic relationships (how's that for alliteration?) tend to take things slow at the beginning. They are more cautious and tend to wait to see who the person that they are trying to win over truly is. Most of their hesitancy is because they are fearful someone will criticize them as much as they criticize themselves. Ones have a difficult time easing into relationships because of their inability to relax at times. Once Ones are able to relax and show their true selves and feelings, they will be extremely loyal to the relationship.

Reformers typically have very specific qualities that they look for in their partner because they know what they want in and out of a relationship. Similarly, they won't compromise their desires and usually have a laundry list of nonnegotiables. This could also create a trouble spot for Ones, as no one is ever perfect and they are constantly searching for what they consider to be the "perfect" partner. This could lead to their partners feeling like they aren't good enough for them or that they could never live up to the high expectations. Romantic partners of Reformers could also feel like they are constantly being criticized or that the One would be better off with someone who has more of the traits they desire. It's important to remember that even if you feel like Ones are criticizing you, they are likely criticizing themselves even more. With a healthy amount of communication and expression of expectations, a romantic relationship with a Reformer can be full of respect, fairness, and truthfulness. You'll never have to wonder where they stand in the relationship, they will always attempt to keep things fair in arguments or disagreements, and your entire household will be running (effectively) on a schedule.

I once met someone who was married to an Enneagram One. He described his partner as someone who "doesn't like to sit down." Full of responsibility, structure, and the need to "get things done," he knew he could fully rely on his partner to be consistent in how they handled their relationship and how they completed household tasks. He said that the conflict they experienced usually involved him not helping with household tasks nor understanding the expectations the One set. The problem was, even though Reformers believe no one will be able to do things quite like them, they still want assistance with tasks—or, if

DATING AN
ENNEAGRAM ONE

Enneagram Ones love structure and organization, and that is the same for dates with their partners as well. Enneagram Ones thrive in environments where they can plan and enjoy planning their own dates, but they like to be surprised every now and then. However, when they are surprised, it needs to be with something that they have experienced before because they know they will enjoy that environment. Ones are also big fans of meaningful conversations and anything that can take their relationship to a deeper level. Specific date ideas for Enneagram Ones could include taking them to their favorite restaurant, playing their favorite games, or an activity connected to hobbies that they enjoy.

not assistance, then recognition for handling everything. Either way, Ones are the partners who are working to constantly perfect the world, and they just want to know that their actions are perceived as "good" and "right" to everyone around them.

Relationships with Family

I like to think of Reformers as people who keep the family together. They are kind of like the glue of the family because of their ability to create structure out of chaos. As with their other relationships, Enneagram Ones value the meaning of family and the connections they have with them. Reformers are usually the leader of the family structure. When they become parents, they are able to take on the new responsibilities and challenges with ease. It's almost like they were made to raise little people: They are good at teaching children how to be ethical and responsible and have good morals—basically, how to be decent human beings. With their strong desire to follow the rules, Reformer parents will follow what they think are the "rules" of parenting.

Because of their perfectionist tendencies, they may struggle with a house that feels chaotic. The stress of maintaining a household can be difficult for them because they could get into a pattern of going, going, going that ultimately leads to burnout. They might feel like they are the only people doing things around the house and could feel resentment toward other family members. They might feel frustrated that others don't care about the typical household chores in the same way they do, not realizing that everyone has different things that they care about.

I see this playing out often with clients I work with in my coaching business. The resentment and frustration comes down to a lack of communication about what everyone expects in a home and in family life. Like I said before, what's "perfect" in the eyes of a Reformer does not necessarily mean completely spotless or clean. That's why it's so important for Ones (and really everyone) to communicate what they need their home life to look and feel like.

Be the Best One You Can Be

Take a deep breath. That was a lot! I hope you're encouraged to see that even though we recognize these character traits in ourselves and others, there is so much room for growth. My biggest piece of advice is to see how this information resonates with you, even the things that make you uncomfortable. You are the *one* to change the things that cause harm to both yourself and others.

FIVE TIPS TO BE YOUR BEST SELF IN THE REAL WORLD

1. Really consider the things you want to do versus the things you feel you should do. Are you doing something because it brings you joy? Or do you feel like there's an expectation?

2. Think about how anger reveals itself in your personality and your interactions with others. When you feel that anger coming on—whether through sarcasm, words, or visible anger—try to think back to the root of the issue.

3. Practice doing things imperfectly—and being okay with it. This will take time, but it will relieve extra pressure and stress.

4. Practice putting yourself in other people's shoes. Thinking about others and their situations can help alleviate some of the judgment and criticism you may subconsciously have.

5. Practicing mindfulness and participating in yoga, Pilates, or other exercise classes can help you relieve stress and focus on how you're feeling at that moment.

PRACTICAL RELATIONSHIP STRATEGIES FOR A REFORMER

1. Learn how to silence your self-critic. You can't be less judgmental of others if you don't practice this with yourself first. You are not going to be perfect. No one is perfect—and that is okay.

2. Learn how to forgive and be kind to yourself.

3. Communication is key. Express encouragement instead of using harsh words. Adjust your tone of voice when you have an urge to respond in a sharp way.

4. When something is upsetting you, be direct with your words and try to avoid letting your anger build up.

5. Recognize that you will not and should not have to change someone. Accept the people in your life just the way that they are, because they are accepting you as you are.

Type

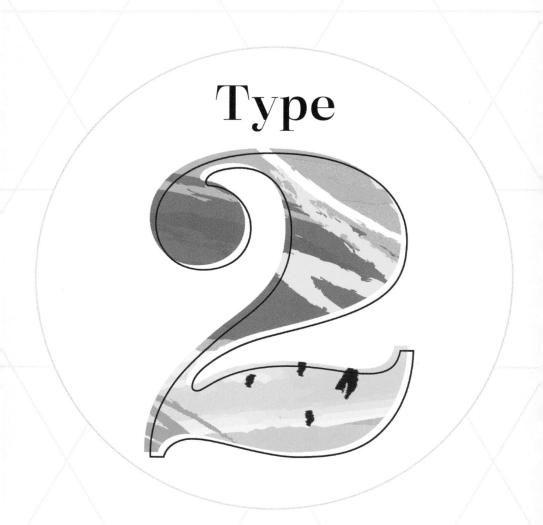

CHAPTER THREE

The Helper

O h, Twos. Sweet, sweet, Twos. This chapter may sting a bit. But we're going to get through it together. *The Helper* is also known as *The Giver* because of their ability to give so much of themselves in the form of words, gifts, acts of service, resources, and time in general. Where Twos can get into trouble, however, is requiring appreciation from others in order to "give." This can lead to unmet expectations, bitterness, and burnout from helping. Their biggest desire is to feel loved and needed, and their biggest fear is to be unwanted in life. Not only is it important for people to understand how to appreciate Enneagram Twos, it's even more important for Twos to learn how to give without receiving anything in return. Throughout this chapter, we will discuss various relationships The Helper may have and how they can navigate them in the healthiest way possible.

Getting to Know The Helper

Helper. Giver. Supporter. Right-hand person. Provider. Those are some words I think of when I think about Enneagram Twos. It exhilarates them to be able to help others, and they live for the validation that they receive from doing acts of kindness. They are kind, generous, and selfless people when they are in a healthy state. However, when they are exhibiting unhealthy qualities of the Two, they can be needy and manipulative and burn out from giving when they neglect their own needs. Here are some other character traits of a Two:

» Loving

» Caring

» Enthusiastic

» Empathetic

» People-pleasing

» Sentimental

» Unselfish

» Patient

» Overly accommodating

» Dependent

Common Mistypes

It is natural for many people to mistype themselves as an Enneagram Two, especially if they are just helpful individuals. However, it is most common for women in general to mistype as a Two because of the social stigma that says women have to be generous, helpful, and caring individuals. Some common mistypes of an Enneagram Two are Types Nine, Seven, and Six. Nines and Twos are one of the most common mistypes because they do seem a lot alike. They both have a desire to please others and are empathetic and kind people. However, Twos want to please others because they want to be loved and wanted. Nines please others because it keeps the peace. Twos and Sevens seem alike because they are both bubbly and outgoing. However, a Two's biggest fear is being disliked, whereas Sevens fear missing out. Finally, Twos and Sixes seem alike because they are both warm and inviting individuals. But

Twos are focused more on receiving acceptance from others, whereas Sixes are mostly focused on certainty and security.

Childhood

As children, Enneagram Twos always have the desire to be loved and wanted. In childhood, they especially want to receive those feelings from authoritative figures in their lives, such as parents and caregivers. These children can often be seen helping around the house, assisting with favors, and doing extra things to be noticed by the people they care about. Twos as children are extremely sensitive to criticism from those they care about—specifically friends, family members, and teachers—and they hold onto criticism for an extended period of time. They typically go along with what other people want to do and want to be seen as helpful and caring kids. Helper children are prone to doing things to gain attention. Have you ever seen kids who always want to wear an elastic wrap bandage? Or the children who are always sick? Sure, they may be injured or sick, but they also just really want someone to notice them. Because we know that our Enneagram type is with us from birth, childhood experiences don't indicate what our Enneagram type will be in the future. So, for example, it's not necessarily that the Enneagram Two was not shown love by their authoritative figures, it's all about their own perceptions.

Worldview

Helpers view the world as if everyone needs something and they personally have what it takes to make each person whole again. They think everyone is going through something and feel that it's their responsibility to make an impact on people, even if it's small. Type Twos are extremely passionate about lightening the burden most people carry and playing a part in making the world a better place.

Strengths and Weaknesses

Like all types, there are many strengths and weaknesses of an Enneagram Two. Twos are extremely connected to other people. This can be perceived as a strength or a weakness, because they often care a little too much about what people think of them. But, by being connected to people, they are able to predict other people's feelings and have a strong read of whatever room they enter. Twos are great listeners, as they take any opportunity to be aware of the needs of others. They are also enthusiastic, fun-loving people. Typically, they are outgoing and will light up every room they enter. They will instantly make your world a happier place because of their generous, loving energy and their inability to allow people to live their lives without the care of a Two. However, that sometimes comes at the expense of Twos taking care of themselves and their own needs. Helpers are known to neglect themselves to continuously help others. One of their biggest struggles is learning how to say no to people when they've reached their limits, as they will continue to insert themselves to feel the validation and appreciation from those closest to them.

Dealing with Conflict

Most Twos dislike conflict because of their fear that it will make them unloved and unwanted. They sometimes have a hard time speaking up about it, and will let others address the conflict first.

Enneagram Two Wings

There are many traits that might affect the way certain Helpers react and respond in relationships. I will remind everyone of the impact of their wings in every single chapter. You may have access to one wing, you may have access to both wings, or you may feel like you don't have access to either wing. However you feel, attempting to pull healthy traits from the wings on either side of your number is important to attaining personal growth. A Two who relies mostly on their One wing will be more

THREE FAMOUS HELPERS

Famous Helpers can be identified because of their desire to help others. Similar to Ones, they could be wanting to help a cause, or simply help individuals.

- Eleanor Roosevelt was an Enneagram Two and is known for being an activist, specifically for civil rights.

- Another famous Helper was Mary Kay Ash from Mary Kay Cosmetics. She built her company from a desire to help women feel better about themselves and comfortable in their skin.

- Nancy Reagan was also an evident Type Two. Although she was known for her cause of the prevention of recreational drug use, she also spent many years devoted to caring for her husband. Nancy Reagan was known as a kind and generous soul.

task-oriented and organized and focus less on what other people think about them. They are much better at saying no than traditional Twos. A Two with a Three wing is a little more outgoing and able to be in the spotlight. They have more of a focus on setting and achieving goals, as well as being seen as valuable and successful. These Twos care more about what other people think of them.

Relationships with The Helper

The three words that come to mind when thinking about being in any sort of relationship with a Helper are sensitivity, selflessness, and affection. If you are in a relationship with an Enneagram Two, prepare to be loved to the fullest and never have a doubt about how they feel about you. Everyone else will also know how they feel about you, because their passion does not stay silent, especially in relationships. Because of their social tendencies, Helpers want to tell the world how they feel about you. Enneagram Twos were made for creating relationships with others, and they do not take them lightly. They go all in, heart-first and with their emotions on their sleeves, ready to change their friends, partners, and family members' lives for the better and help them along the way while doing it.

When I say that Type Twos are sensitive, I mean they are extremely sensitive to the needs of those around them. It doesn't matter if the needs are physical or emotional: Helpers will be able to identify and respond to the needs of those with whom they are in relationships. Helpers are also known to be very sensitive in general. They will most likely take offense to any sort of criticism, even if it is meant to be constructive. It always goes back to their desire to be wanted and loved, because Twos feel that if they're being criticized, they are not wanted in that space. They feel everything deeply, and their sensitivity demonstrates that.

Enneagram Twos are the epitome of showing just how selfless human beings can be when they're in a healthy place. They will always put the needs of others before their own because they are motivated by moving others toward a place of stability and growth. However, Helpers can sometimes become "too selfless," where they neglect their needs entirely. Twos have a tendency to think about others so much that they forget they have their own priorities and then they can't save themselves. They also tend to hold their own feelings inside because they only want to hear the needs and burdens of others. This selflessness can be an amazing quality of Enneagram Twos, but they need to find a balance between taking care of others and taking care of themselves.

Affection plays a key role in all relationships with Enneagram Twos. This doesn't necessarily mean physical affection, but the art of showing others just how much they mean to them. Affection can be defined as "the act or process of affecting or being affected." Helpers will affect others in multiple ways. They could have a positive influence on others, they could show kindness when they are in a state of despair, or they could just offer a smile on a bad day. Twos will also show you how you are affecting them, because the act of receiving affection is very important for a Two's well-being and motivation to move forward in life. When in a relationship with a Helper, it's necessary to realize that affection will be a central aspect of the pairing. Friends, partners, family members, anyone, prepare to receive affection.

Relationships with Colleagues

It is hard to be an Enneagram Two in the workplace. Let's just call it what it is. People are not required to like you at work. Twos will most likely be criticized at some point, even if it is just constructive criticism. There will be conflict that Twos may have to address every now and then, and that is uncomfortable for them. It's obviously doable, and it is so important to seek to understand how Twos interact in the workplace. Helpers are quick to receive validation that their coworkers, supervisors, and colleagues like them and want to work with them. They tend to need more validation than other Enneagram types and are typically more dependent than other types. However, this is an area in which it's important that their supervisor encourages them to grow. Twos have to learn that they don't need everyone to like them and that they can stand on their own two feet. Despite these negative qualities, Twos are fantastic at helping and assisting with projects in the workplace. However, their desire to please others will often have them signing up for more than they can handle.

Joanna, an Enneagram Three (The Achiever), has a coworker who is an Enneagram Two. She recognizes that both types are fairly similar, as Two desires to be wanted and Three wants to be seen as valuable. However, the main difference between them is the validation that her coworker needs. Her coworker always wanted to be told she was doing a good job. Joanna watched her Helper coworker always say yes to assisting with projects on their team. Even though Joanna was initially happy that it lightened her load, she worried that her coworker would burn out. That's exactly what happened when the Helper realized that she had too much on her plate. By reminding her coworker that she doesn't need to always help out, Joanna was able to remove some things from her coworker's to-do list and is helping her work toward a healthy state of living and working.

Relationships with Friends

People love being friends with Twos. They are generally easy to get along with, playful, kind, and extremely nurturing. Twos as friends are just how you would imagine them to be. They are the friend who is always there for you, the one you call when you're going through a breakup or need to hear the great things they love about you. Enneagram Twos are always willing to help you out, whether it's watching your child, pet sitting for you, or offering to drive you somewhere. However, despite all of these amazing qualities, they do have some downfalls in friendships. As you can imagine, a Two in an unhealthy headspace can become pretty jealous of their friends having friendships with other people. It's not that they actually care about the other people specifically; it's that they are afraid you will not love them as much as you love your new friends. Reassure them that you still feel the same way about them and that your friendship will not falter even as you form new friendships.

I can best describe this by telling you a story about Amanda. Amanda has many friends and most of them happen to be Enneagram Sevens (The Enthusiast). Sevens and Twos can actually look pretty similar, as they are both outgoing and part of the optimist triad. As we know, a Two's main desire is to feel loved and wanted, whereas a Seven's is to feel content. Twos are satisfied staying at home sometimes and having one-on-one time with friends. Sevens like to keep exploring to find the next best thing. Amanda's group of Enthusiast friends always like to go on adventures and are professionals at doing things at the last minute and being spontaneous. Amanda has a hard time with that and often feels like she's left out of social situations. The thing is, the root of a Two feeling that way is because they feel unwanted. I know, it sounds illogical. I encouraged Amanda to talk to her friends about how she was feeling and to work on compromising at times but also learning how to step out of her comfort zone. That need to feel wanted is so strong for Type Twos.

Romantic Relationships

Enneagram Twos are good at making their partners feel loved and wanted in relationships because that's exactly how they want to feel. They are attentive to their partner's needs, great at

DATING AN
ENNEAGRAM TWO

Enneagram Twos are not used to other people taking care of them. They are familiar with catering their wants and needs to the other person. Because they are so focused on the relationship itself, Enneagram Twos enjoy dates that are specifically related to spending time with their partner. They don't necessarily care about what they are doing, just about who they are spending time with in that moment. It's important that you listen to what a Two might want to do, but more importantly to spend that time with them, listening and showing them that you care. When deciding the specific date to go on with your Enneagram Two, listen closely to the needs and wants of your partner. Choose based on that, and remember that just the simple act of being together is enough for them.

asking them how their day was, and alarmingly good at predicting their feelings. However, if Twos are demonstrating some of the unhealthy characteristics of their type, they can be considered clingy and a little too devoted to their partner. If Twos are in an unhealthy place in their lives, they tend to be controlling and possessive and want to keep their partners to themselves. Because they aren't very good at discussing their feelings and needs, they can become manipulative to get their partner to figure out what they really want. However, Twos in a healthy state make excellent companions because they put others' needs before their own and love fully and deeply.

An Enneagram Two I know named April spoke to me about some realizations she had about her type. She said that she could think back on time periods of her life when she demonstrated the manipulation and possessiveness I mentioned previously. Her husband, Derek, is an Enneagram Six (The Loyalist), and she feels like they make a pretty exceptional pair. April is a bit more outgoing and chaotic, and Derek is stable and a little quieter. However, she recognizes that Twos in relationships can definitely smother other people with their love and helpfulness. There are times when Derek wants April to help him, but she acknowledged that he definitely needs his time by himself. Relationships with Twos can be very successful with communication, healthy boundaries, and learned independence.

Relationships with Family

Enneagram Twos in families are usually helping people with everything. They may be hosting people for a meal, helping with homework, or surprising family members with gifts. It brings them immense joy to do all of these things. Helper parents can be identified because of the way they love and encourage their children. They are attentive, affectionate, and devoted to their family members. Twos are often extremely protective of their family and will do what it takes to make sure that they feel wanted and loved at all times. However, that is also usually the cause of Enneagram Twos worrying constantly about whether they are doing enough for their family members. Twos always want to make sure that their family members are happy and not mad at them.

As I mentioned in the Introduction, I'm a Two. I think it's also valuable to share how I interacted with my family growing up. When I was younger, I didn't know the Enneagram. But now, looking back, I'm able to see just how much I acted like a Two. I was a rule-follower (probably my One wing) but was totally driven by pleasing my parents. Whereas Ones follow rules because that's what you're "supposed" to do in life, I (a Two) would follow my parents' rules so they would love and want me. All my mom had to do was say that she was disappointed in me and I would crumble and be heartbroken. Twos in families just want to please everyone.

Be the Best Two You Can Be

Okay Twos, time to take a deep breath again. Learning this information can be particularly difficult because Enneagram Twos don't handle constructive criticism well. The best way to process this information is to take it in, think about it, and grow through it. The pieces that make you feel uncomfortable (or perhaps even slightly nauseated) are usually the areas that you need to focus on. Take it one step at a time and pretty soon you won't even identify with the unhealthy characteristics of a Two.

FIVE TIPS TO BE YOUR BEST SELF IN THE REAL WORLD

1. Work on saying no. This may be hard, and it will take some practice, but it's time to commit only to the things that make you the happiest. It's also important that you learn to do things simply for yourself.

2. Refrain from helping people when they clearly don't want to be helped. Wait for people to ask for your help so you don't insert yourself where you aren't needed (or wanted).

3. Don't try to be the rescuer. Ugh, this is so hard! You cannot always pull people out of their troubles and problems, and sometimes they do not want help with them.

4. Find a career that you're passionate about and be vocal about your own needs. Don't expect other people to automatically know what you need from them.

5. Set limits at work and decide what is really for you to do. Don't volunteer to complete tasks that aren't a part of your job description, and watch for burnout when you take on too much.

PRACTICAL RELATIONSHIP STRATEGIES FOR A HELPER

1. Remember that you will be okay, even without external validation.

2. Take things slowly in romantic relationships. Remember who you are outside of the relationship, in any kind of relationship. This can be hard for some Twos because they may define themselves by the relationships they are in.

3. Set aside time for yourself to simply serve you. Learn how to please yourself instead of others.

4. Identify when you feel the "guilt trip" coming on. Remember that those close to you will show love in ways you may not be used to receiving, but that doesn't mean that they love you any less.

5. Who are you when you're not helping your partner? Really look to discover who you are as an individual.

Type

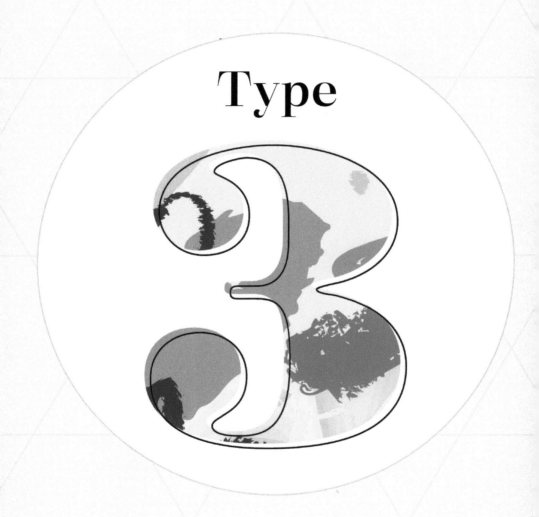

CHAPTER FOUR

The Achiever

Enneagram Three is known as *The Achiever.* Some Enneagram experts also refer to this type as *The Performer* because of their ability to always know how they need to act or "perform" to be seen in a certain way by those around them. Achievers are known for their strong motivation to reach their goals, and they will do what they must to get there. Achievers have many great qualities, including efficiency, positivity, and being hardworking. Threes can get in trouble when they become overzealous and extremely into themselves and their abilities. Enneagram Threes are also a part of the competency triad. Enneagram types in this triad value being seen as competent, and Threes specifically value achieving success once they put their mind to a task. Type Three's biggest fear is being seen as worthless, whereas their biggest desire is for their life to be valuable and worthwhile. Let's explore Type Threes together and learn how to interact and grow with this relationship.

Getting to Know The Achiever

Achiever. Performer. Doer. Go-Getter. Wheeler and dealer. All of these words and phrases could be accurate titles for Enneagram Threes. The Achiever is defined as a person who attains a high level of success. It could also be whatever success means to that person. Yes, Achievers are focused on success. But they are not only focused on achieving their own success, they also love being able to help others attain whatever goal they are trying to achieve. The Achiever likes to be the best at everything that they do, which can be detrimental because they might jump into the pattern of always thinking they are better than others. Here are some other traits that describe Threes:

» Optimistic

» Goal-oriented

» Focused

» Charming

» Outgoing

» Driven

» Motivated

» Energetic

» Confident

» Image-conscious

» Charismatic

Common Mistypes

People often mistype themselves as an Enneagram Three if they generally consider themselves to be goal-oriented, motivated, and focused on achievements. Obviously, anyone can have those traits and characteristics, and the most common mistypes of a Three are Types Eight, Seven, and Five. Threes and Eights are often mistyped because they are both assertive and have the tendency to take charge. However, Threes take charge because they want to be seen as valuable, whereas Eights just want to be in control. Threes and Sevens seem similar because they are both typically outgoing and fun-loving. The main differences between them, however, is that Threes care a lot about the way people see them, whereas Sevens are more "go with the flow." Finally, Threes and Fives seem similar because they both have a strong work ethic and ability to get things done. The main difference is that Threes love to stand out, whereas Fives want nothing more than to blend in.

Childhood

Enneagram Threes as children can often be confused with Enneagram Ones because of their desire to be perfect. But the motivation behind their perfection is that they want to be seen as valuable to the caregivers in their lives, whereas Type Ones just want to be seen as good. Enneagram Three children want their caregivers to see that they have something to offer them, whereas Ones want to be the prized child. Threes as children are always trying to gain the attention of relatives, loved ones, and people important to them by stating or demonstrating their achievements. Achiever children want to be appreciated more than any other number on the Enneagram, and not only appreciated for who they are, but specifically for what they have accomplished. These children are involved in many activities in their school or community. But here's the thing: They don't know when to stop. This is because if they are receiving the attention for their accomplishments, they will continue to chase that feeling. Achiever children can burn out quickly from having so many after-school activities because it limits their free time with friends. Because of their charismatic personality, Type Three children are usually well-liked by their peers, teachers, and authoritative figures. This expands past childhood and can contribute to the Threes' need to be liked by others.

Worldview

Achievers view the world as if there is a result to everything. What I mean by this is that they think that the purpose of doing activities is to see results. Going to work? It's to do a good job. Going to the gym? It's not just a casual thing because they're into fitness. They work out to get results. Want to become a parent? You better believe Achievers want to be the best parent there ever was and raise the best and most perfect child. Achievers believe that it is up to them to attain results.

Strengths and Weaknesses

Enneagram Threes have many strengths, especially when it comes to efficiency and motivation. Achievers are naturally optimistic people, which makes it difficult for them to be in the presence of negativity. Not only are they fantastic self-motivators, but they are also really great at pushing others to be the best they can be. You can typically spot a Type Three in a crowd because of their charismatic personality and ability to speak to anyone about literally any topic on the planet. Most Threes are extremely outgoing and skilled storytellers. Despite all of these positive attributes, there are always some negative traits that can sneak in there if we aren't living out the healthy sides of our types. Threes can be known for being a bit self-focused because they want to be seen as the absolute best at whatever they do. Threes are also known to put their job (whatever it is, not necessarily a traditional nine-to-five) before anything else because the idea of success is the most important thing to them. Achievers have the ability to be perceived as whoever they need to be. They are often described as chameleons because they can change their personality to get others to like and want to be around them. Threes need to be reminded to remain true to who they are because, if not, they will continue to be who other people want them to be, which can be extremely exhausting to those around them.

Dealing with Conflict

Enneagram Threes do one of two things: They either act like it never happened and go on with their lives, or they feel comfortable going straight to the source. Because Threes are so focused on appearances, their decision will be based on what makes them look better to other people.

THREE FAMOUS ACHIEVERS

You can determine famous Achievers by their inability to stop chasing their dreams and climbing the ladder of success.

- Someone who is clearly an Enneagram Three is Arnold Schwarzenegger. Schwarzenegger rose to fame with his acting career through his role in the *Terminator* series. However, he didn't stop there. He continued to try to be the best bodybuilder, the best actor, and ultimately became the governor of California. He never wanted to stop being the best at whatever he accomplished.

- Another famous Enneagram Three is Taylor Swift, one of the most successful artists of our time. She is an incredible songwriter, has excelled as a businessperson, and is generous with her success.

- Another Type Three is Oprah Winfrey. She overcame extreme adversity and created her own talk show, which became the highest-rated show of its kind. What makes her a healthy Three is that she is also well-known as a philanthropist, giving back to people and communities because of her success.

Enneagram Three Wings

The wings for Achievers can make a Three look completely different. It's so interesting to me how many different personalities are within an Enneagram type. A Three with a stronger Two wing (The Helper) is going to be more generous, empathetic, and more sociable than Threes who rely more heavily on their Four wing (The Individualist). The Two wing will also be more of an encourager to their peers and those around them. In contrast, a Three with more access to the Four wing will be more artistic and more focused on their feelings. They may be more sensitive, quiet, and creative. If a Three has balanced wings, they will be able to rely on qualities from both Twos and Fours, and be well-rounded with traits like generosity, creativity, sensitivity, and being goal-oriented.

Relationships with The Achiever

Relationships with The Achiever are typically filled with social situations and are playful and charming. Achievers are extremely charismatic. If you are in any type of relationship with an Enneagram Three, you experience their radiating energy. This energy is usually contagious, so shared activities may include house projects, competitive sports or races, or spending your weekends checking things off your bucket list. Even though some Achievers may present as introverted, they will still have a seemingly endless amount of energy to get things done and may need to recharge in a different way than extroverted Achievers. This type in relationships can be similar to Enneagram Seven; however, Sevens enjoy checking things off of their bucket list because of the adventure it brings, whereas Threes feel valuable because they accomplished it.

Achievers are extremely social. They are comfortable at events that require conversation and attention to others. They also typically don't have an issue sparking up conversation with a total stranger. Whether you're in a friend, romantic, familial, or work relationship with a Three, you can almost guarantee that it will be full of social activities. This could be defined as going out somewhere for dinner or an activity or simply having game nights at home. Achievers value this social interaction with other people.

Another trait of Achievers in relationships is their playful and fun demeanor. Type Threes are typically loud with an extensive sense of humor. They are known to be "class clowns," always cracking jokes and trying to make others laugh. They will be a ton of fun to be around in general. Enneagram Threes are playful in a way that they know others want to receive it. Meaning, if they know you like jokes, then they'll crack jokes all day long. If they know you like to be surprised, they'll make sure that they throw the best surprise ever. Everything is all about being seen as the "best," no matter what they do. Even though it's important they are seen as competent, they don't take life too seriously. Sure, they have serious moments at times. But when they do stress, they take on traits of an Enneagram Nine, the most laid-back number on the Enneagram. Achievers are naturally happy and playful people in all of their interactions with people.

When I say that Type Threes are "charming," I'm not talking about Prince Charming coming to save the day. (Although Achievers could also do that, I suppose.) Achievers are charming in the way that they know what they have to do to make others like them and enjoy being in their presence. They know how to act, what to say, and how to react. This isn't necessarily a bad thing; it just happens to be a skill that not many people have. It can, however, turn into a negative trait when Threes forget who they are because they are always being someone else. In relationships, though, this trait comes into play when Threes are trying to fit into different social settings. Whether in friend, romantic, or work relationships, Achievers know who to be and what they need to do to get there.

Relationships with Colleagues

Buckle in, colleagues of Threes. Prepare to always feel like you just can't compete with your Achiever coworker. This is because they will always appear to have everything in check, even if they absolutely do not have it together. That's the key thing about Threes. Appearances, appearances, appearances. Sure, there are some Type Threes who are definitely on track to meet their goals and succeed at their job. But there are also Threes who you may think are succeeding when they actually are not. It's just the perception. However, one thing is guaranteed to be prevalent in Achievers in the workplace: goals. That's right. Goal setting, goal planning, achieving goals, small goals, large goals, completely unattainable goals. Goals are pretty much a Three's best friend because they are extremely focused on their career. You can typically spot your Type Three coworker because they are staying late, checking their email on weekends, and never working less than 40 hours in a week. Whatever their career, they are all in. If you're all in with them, then great. If not, then sit on the sidelines and watch them accomplish everything at their job.

Julia has many Enneagram Threes in her life, and here's the cool thing about that: They are all different. They all have different professions, different values and things that they care about, and different personalities. But here is the thing she stated that they all have in common: They are all extremely hardworking. Let me tell you about her brother, Steve. He's three years older than her, and she thinks he created his first vision board when she was still in middle school. Focused on success, he knew where he wanted to go to college, what he wanted to study, and what he wanted the rest of his life to look like. Recently he made a pretty massive career change and decided to start working for their dad (also a Three) at the family business. It's a huge risk, but one her brother knew he could take because that's just how he is. Achievers are natural leaders, and you will most likely see them in charge of something.

Relationships with Friends

When you are friends with an Enneagram Three, it's important to be intentional about planning to spend time together. This is because Threes are so focused on everything else, sometimes they can neglect the relationships closest to them. This is not intentional—their one-track mind is just focused on succeeding at their goals. You taking the initiative on planning your gathering could be very helpful for them because it's one less thing they have to worry about. Threes love any activity that is some sort of competition. They might not actually think that they are competitive, but then you'll go miniature golfing and it will be obvious to everyone. Additionally, showing appreciation for your Achiever friend is going to be the most important thing you can do. Remember, Threes want to be valued, so it's important that you show them just how valuable they are to you.

There is an Achiever named Christina who is in a friend group with a Two (The Helper), a Four (The Individualist), and an Eight (The Challenger). Sometimes her friends are upset with her because she doesn't always make time for them and doesn't do well with a spur-of-the-moment request for a happy hour. She needs things to be planned weeks in advance. When they do get together, Christina typically shows up late because she was finishing up tasks at her job. Her friends get upset she's late, but Christina feels upset that they don't see how important her job is to her. The problem here is really a breakdown in communication. This is one of the reasons I love the Enneagram. If all parties in this situation would communicate what they want, need, and desire based on their Enneagram type, conflict could be avoided. However, Threes need to be intentional about setting aside time for the relationships closest to them or they may unintentionally exclude others from their lives.

Romantic Relationships

Threes are intense romantic partners, it should be said. But all in the best ways possible! They push you to achieve greatness and want to climb the success ladder right next to you. Threes in romantic relationships need to feel valuable to their partners, and they think they need to do things to receive those feelings. This means your Three partner might constantly be on the go, working late, and doing things to better themselves and your family, which is fine, as long as there's a balance between caring for the relationship and caring for themselves. Keep in mind that appearances are extremely important to Threes. This means they like to conceal potential relationship issues, which can sometimes lead to sweeping issues under the rug and not dealing with them head-on. This can also happen when Threes get stressed out due to the integration to their stress line, which connects them with the qualities of Enneagram Nine (The Peacemaker). However, Achievers are at their best in relationships when they also value their partners, are extremely helpful, and push their partners toward their goals in a kind and supportive way.

Shawn (a Three) and Ashley (a One) have been married for five years and have two young children. I've had the opportunity to gain insight into their relationship from speaking with both of them and having an outside perspective. The key difference here is that Threes respond with feelings, whereas Ones respond with anger—though not always outward. This means communication and understanding could be difficult between the two of them. Threes respond to situations with feelings, but they aren't exceptionally good at showing how they feel about other people. Shawn is the perfect example of this. He has very strong, romantic feelings about Ashley but isn't always good at showing it. However, Shawn is extremely outgoing, humorous, and playful in their relationship, and feels like that is showing his feelings. If you're in a relationship with an Achiever, prepare to

DATING AN ENNEAGRAM THREE

Enneagram Threes thrive on excitement and competition, and it's no different for the dates they go on with their partners. Dates with Enneagram Threes should be focused around activities. Obviously it's important to know what kinds of activities your Enneagram Three enjoys doing, but activity-focused is the key. This could look like trying a new restaurant, going on a hike, or something competition-based like an escape room. Anything with competition is bound to go over well.

experience radiating energy and an intense desire to be seen as successful in every aspect of their lives, and yes, that includes romantic relationships.

Relationships with Family

Two words describe a father who is a Three: dad jokes. And you better believe they will be the best dad jokes ever. In general, Enneagram Threes as parents will make sure their children are doing and being the best they can be, wearing the best and latest trends, and getting great grades at school. Remember, it's all about appearances. Achiever parents need to be careful about the amount of pressure they put on their children to be the best. While you won't know what your child's Enneagram type is yet, it's especially important to be careful of criticism when you have a sensitive child who wants to please you. Excessive pressure can cause heartbreak and stress. It's also important to practice showing your true self in front of your children, or they may feel like they have to pretend to be someone they're not. Healthy Achievers in family relationships are loyal, cheering everyone on and ensuring that their success is best for the entire family.

I have a friend whose parents are Threes. Yes, both parents! The house was always full of friendly (and sometimes not so friendly) competition. Races, sporting events, family game nights—you name it. She learned to love the competition but felt a lot of pressure growing up. If she didn't get an A on a test, she was pushed hard by both parents to get an A next time. Because she has a bit of an obsessive personality, this would lead to her spending an excessive amount of time studying. But no matter what happened, she never felt good enough. Her grades, where she went to college, her career choice, her lifestyle—she never felt like she could quite achieve things the way her parents could. Eventually, she was able to tell them how she felt about it, and their relationships have improved. But this is the perfect example of how enormous pressure could impact a family relationship.

Be the Best Three You Can Be

Threes, relationships with you can be amazing because you will always strive to be the best you can be, and that feels comfortable for you. Just remember to work on being yourself so people can see the real you. Don't feel discouraged for wearing the mask—just take these words and put them into action. The world needs to see you and hear you and be in relationships of all kinds with Enneagram Threes.

FIVE TIPS TO BE YOUR BEST SELF IN THE REAL WORLD

1. Unplug from your work responsibilities every now and then. This can look different for everyone, but I'm talking generally about closing your laptop, not checking work emails on the weekend, and not saying yes to tasks that aren't for you.

2. Practice being instead of doing, which can be hard. Be present with your loved ones because they love you for you, not for what you can accomplish.

3. Really think about who you are when you take off the mask. Who are you when people aren't telling you who to be? Who do you want to be versus who others want you to be?

4. Focus on others' achievements. This may be difficult because Threes are constantly focusing on their own accomplishments, but seek out those who have achieved great things recently and let them know.

5. Be diligent about recognizing traits in yourself that you don't like. Focus on changing those traits to be a better you.

PRACTICAL RELATIONSHIP STRATEGIES FOR AN ACHIEVER

1. Be diligent about scheduling one-on-one time with your partner and each of your friends. They may feel like you don't spend enough time with them, so it's important you make an effort to do just that.

2. Remember that your partner is with you because they love you for who you are. Don't try to be someone you aren't. Focus on what brought you together in the first place.

3. Practice intentional listening without giving your own advice. Sometimes people just need to vent or tell you about their day, so it's important that you respect them enough to do that.

4. Remember how much your partner does for you. You aren't the only one bringing things into the relationship. Show them how much you appreciate them and their accomplishments.

5. Remember that you don't always have to be the best. Allow your partner to do things for you, encourage them to be good at things, and focus on equality between the two of you.

Type

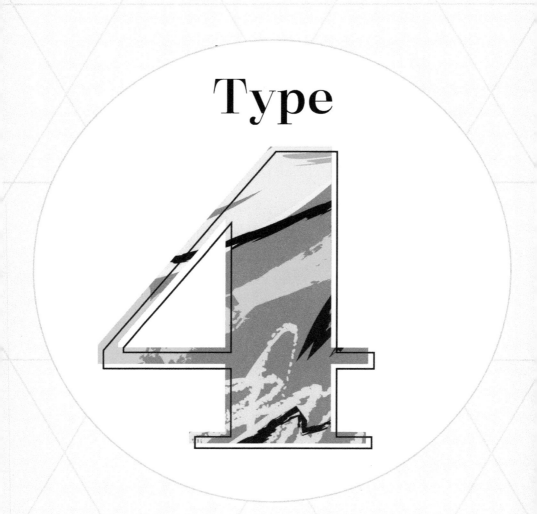

CHAPTER FIVE

The Individualist

Τhe *Individualist. The Romantic.* The most unique type on the Enneagram, Fours are the most misunderstood yet are dying to *be* understood. And known. And loved. And cared for. Fours, it's your turn. Fours are extremely motivated by the need to feel known and avoid feeling ordinary. When they are at their best, they are empathetic, warm, friendly, and very creative. But sometimes their emotions can get the best of them, and they can take on some unhealthy qualities, such as being moody, stubborn, self-absorbed, attention-seeking, and having an almost "woe is me" attitude. Often, Fours feel like something is very wrong with them, which in turn leads to them feeling even more misunderstood. It's time to do a deep dive into how Fours interact and respond in all types of relationships.

Getting to Know The Individualist

The Individualist is defined as "a person who is independent and self-reliant." This is ultimately what a Four strives to be. Some Enneagram experts refer to Fours as The Romantic because of their intense feelings and emotions for other people. Another personality trait typically prevalent in Fours is their creative and artistic ability. Fours have a way of tapping into their deep feelings and emotions to convey the meaning of life and existence in an artistic and powerful way. Fours want to be seen as unique and different from those around them. They typically are not into things that are considered "mainstream," popular music, or trends. They like to be unique and want others to understand and respect that individuality—that is always their main goal. Here are other traits that describe Fours:

» Sensitive

» Self-aware

» Authentic

» Deep

» Artistic

» Melancholic

» Passionate

» Supportive

» Compassionate

» Warm

» Envious

» Inspiring

» Friendly

Common Mistypes

Many people mistype others as Fours if that person has a single creative bone in their body. That's because Fours are the most artistic Enneagram type. However, many people who aren't Fours are also extremely creative and artistic. The most common mistypes with a Four are Enneagrams Nine, Seven, and Six. Fours and Nines seem similar because they both have an extreme amount of empathy toward others. Fours don't necessarily hate conflict because conflict can be associated with emotion. Nines, on the other hand, will do whatever they can to avoid conflict. Fours and Sevens seem similar because both types are very focused on what they want out of life, and both types can also be very intense. The main difference is that Fours like to sit with their emotions and negativity, whereas Sevens will do whatever they can to avoid feeling emotional pain. Fours and Sixes seem alike because they both spend a lot of time doubting themselves. However, Fours focus on feelings and what could be missing from their lives, whereas Sixes focus on their thoughts and what could go wrong in their lives.

Childhood

Enneagram Fours as children are easily identified because of their elaborate and detailed imaginations. They have had a creative streak from day one, and they let that show by wanting to do artistic activities like crafts, finger painting, or sculpting with Play-Doh. They also might be more sensitive than other children and may be quick to be able to identify what they are feeling and why they are feeling that way. They will most likely even call out feelings and emotions in their friends and class-mates and recognize when they are feeling sad. This is what develops empathy in them later on. However, these children will also feel like they are misunderstood or outcasts at school, in their family, or in social circles. They can get stuck in the com-parison trap, always wishing that they could have what others have, or do what others do. These children would benefit from their parents being intentional about developing social skills and relationships.

Worldview

Individualists view the world as a place to create meaningful connections with others. If connections aren't being made, then their ideal world isn't being fulfilled. Individualists make it their mission to establish deep connections with those who are in their lives. Individualists have this desire to create connections because they can often feel like it's impossible to make them, due to the feeling that they can't relate to others because of their uniqueness and individuality. If they can successfully connect with others, then and only then will they truly understand them.

Strengths and Weaknesses

Individualists have many strengths when it comes to their behaviors and their motivations behind their actions. They are extremely empathetic and sensitive to others' needs. They can relate to others' hardships like no other type, often even shedding tears alongside them. Fours are also always able to experience and enjoy life's little pleasures. Sunsets. Fall leaves. Scents. Rainy days. They can find joy and meaning in just about anything. Fours are known for being extremely creative and artistic, and they use those skills to create meaning in the world. Individualists are very comfortable sitting with their feelings, and even enjoy a little bit (or a lot) of melancholy. This could also be considered a weakness if they are always sitting with their negative feelings. Sometimes those feelings can take them into a deep, dark place, and it can be hard for them to get out of it. Another weakness of Individualists is envy. Fours can feel envious of others when they have what the Four wants or are experiencing things that the Four wants to experience. The interesting thing about this is that they never want to be like anyone else. However, that envy can creep up and cause damage in their relationships with others and themselves. Working on growing through your Enneagram type can help ensure that strengths are more apparent than weaknesses.

Dealing with Conflict

Because Enneagram Fours are so in tune with their emotions, they handle conflict in a similar fashion. Once introduced to the conflict, they will react with their feelings first. This may look different to each Enneagram Four. Some people may withdraw to protect their emotions, while others may deal with it immediately.

THREE FAMOUS INDIVIDUALISTS

Many famous Individualists are in some sort of creative field as artists, actors, or musicians.

- Vincent van Gogh is considered to be an Enneagram Four, and it is so clear why. Obviously, he was an amazingly talented artist, but he was using art as his outlet for his intense feelings of depression and despair. Not all Enneagram Fours suffer from manic episodes like Vincent van Gogh, but I can't help but wonder what would have happened if he was able to use the Enneagram to grow through some of those experiences.

- Another famous Individualist is Edgar Allen Poe, a writer credited with popularizing writing in a short story format. He is best known for his melancholic and mysterious poetry, which demonstrates the qualities of a Type Four.

- Finally, I'd like to introduce you to my man, James Taylor. I have always been deeply interested with who he is as a songwriter and musician, and now as an Enneagram Four. He is an incredible lyricist and creative musician, and his songs tell a story of a man who has always felt a little misunderstood by those around him.

Enneagram Four Wings

Continuing with the color metaphor, let's imagine that Individualists are gray. How many shades of gray are there in the world? Yes, more than just 50. That's how different Fours can be depending on their wings. Fours with a stronger Three wing, called The Aristocrat, will be more driven, goal-oriented, and focused on their accomplishments. They are also more outgoing and ambitious than Fours with more of a Five wing. A Four with more access to the Five wing, called The Bohemian, will be quieter and more introverted than other Fours. They are more withdrawn, more reserved, and typically more focused on academics or the intellectual side of life.

Relationships with The Individualist

Relationships with Individualists can be confusing at first but extremely rewarding. They are confusing because Individualists want to be noticed and to fit in, but they also want to be unique. They often long for what others have, but they are also extremely attuned to the little pleasures of their lives. Fours can keep relationships interesting, for sure. A few words that describe Fours in relationships are empathetic, passionate, and authentic. Let's explore how Fours exhibit these three traits.

Individualists are extremely empathetic. I think it's important to note the difference between empathy and sympathy. Sympathy is feeling sorry for someone (Fours often demonstrate that, too), whereas empathy is being able to actually feel what others are going through. It's walking alongside someone while they are experiencing something. It's taking on the emotions and feelings someone else has. Fours exhibit this trait in relationships by being a huge support system for everyone around them. They will always want to know how they can be there for the people in their lives and bring them back to a better place physically and emotionally. They pride themselves in feeling—and feeling hard. And they won't stop until they can feel your emotions, too.

Along with being empathetic toward people in their lives, they are also extremely passionate. Some Enneagram experts call this type The Romantic because of their intense feelings for desire and romance. Passion is what comes out when Enneagram Fours feel all of the feels—not just for romantic relationships, but in any and all kinds of relationships. Fours can feel passionate about their friendships, their relationships at work, and, of course, relationships with their romantic partners. The passion is just displayed differently in each relationship. For their friends, Fours are passionate about making sure their friends are okay, maintaining those relationships, and being a support system. Passion in their work relationships is typically related to the work itself. Passion in romantic relationships can be displayed in the things mentioned previously, but also in a desire to truly be known and understood by their partner and to be close to them, because that is true intimacy to a Four.

Individualists strive to be as authentic as possible in their relationships. They are driven by authenticity. What this means in relationships is that what you see is what you get. Fours will never try to be someone they're not, and this is also the case in relationships. They won't pretend that their relationship with you is something it's not. Fours want to make sure that people really see them for who they are. They don't want to be compared to someone else because they see themselves as extremely unique. They want you to see them as authentic and to understand who they really are. You'll never have to wonder where you stand in a friendship or romantic relationship with an Individualist. They will always be sure to let you know.

Relationships with Colleagues

Professional relationships in work settings with Individualists can be difficult and hard to understand. Much like other relationships with Fours, people may be left feeling that they don't really understand their coworker. On the other side of that, Fours will feel like they are misunderstood in the workplace, which can cause a toxic environment if there is too little communication. Fours can be extremely compassionate, and they can pick up on the feelings of their coworkers. They are quick to tell you that it's okay to feel emotions if you feel let down at work, or to just feel in general if something is upsetting you. If Individualists are feeling hurt by something a coworker said or did, they will withdraw to sit with their emotions by themselves. It's important you don't push them to "get over it" and also to try not to take those situations personally.

I could see this most clearly when I was speaking to someone who works with an Enneagram Four at a small advertising firm. David was talking to me about this new coworker and how he and his other coworkers just couldn't quite figure the person out. I asked him what he meant by that, and he said that there was just some element of mystery to his coworker, how one minute they seemed to open up, then suddenly were back to withdrawing and not joining in when the rest of the team did things together. David also said that he notices it most often when someone has had a new idea for a marketing campaign that his coworker didn't have. Their team had just gone through an Enneagram training, and he wanted to know how he could best support his coworker, knowing that they were an Enneagram Four. In this situation, it's likely The Individualist coworker was experiencing their "deadly sin"—envy. When The Individualist notices someone else in their workplace excelling at something that they aren't, envy can sneak in, enhance their emotions, and cause them to withdraw. I encouraged David to help them get out of that shell and also encourage them to express why they may be feeling a certain way. Always seek to understand, especially with Individualists. They need to see the effort.

Relationships with Friends

Individualists bring so much creativity and excitement into their friendships because of their unique personalities and dispositions. Relationships are extremely important to Fours, so they will value the friendship you have with them. They care most about deep and meaningful relationships, so they won't have a lot of friends just to say that they do. They will be friends with the people who offer up those deep and meaningful experiences for them. They love to have serious conversations to hear perspectives on different topics, but they can also be lighthearted and enjoy doing activities with those who are closest to them. They are unique, and they will probably be the most unique and original friendship you have. Your other friends may even be confused about your relationship with The Individualist, because they won't understand them. But as long as you seek to understand their originality and perspective on life, they will always value your special friendship.

As I was writing this section, I immediately thought about one of my mom's best friends, Audrey. Audrey has been in our life for quite some time, and I have always viewed her (and her family) as part of our family, too. A single chat with Audrey, and her Individualist nature shines through. A true Individualist, Audrey cares deeply about her friendships, and it brings her to tears just thinking about them. My mom has a tiny bit of Four in her, as her main type is a Three, but nothing compared to Audrey. One of their favorite things to do together is to ask each other meaningful questions. They both (and some of their other friends) spend time thinking of deep and meaningful questions to ask each other, and then they listen and wait with bated breath for the answers. Besides this serious example of time spent together, Audrey has a quirky sense of humor, which leaves her friends wondering how and why she says the things she does. She wants to be different. She wants to be set apart. That's why.

Type 4

Romantic Relationships

Much like other relationships, Fours bring a quirky, one-of-a-kind personality to a romantic relationship. When they are at their healthiest in relationships, they are extremely empathetic and sensitive to their partners' needs and desires. Remember, one of the other titles for this type is The Romantic, and it's obvious why in these types of relationships. Fours bring an immense amount of passion and friendliness, and an ability to create impactful bonds with their romantic partners. I think it's important to also think about some potential areas of concern if Fours are in an unhealthy place with their Enneagram type. When Fours are under stress, they take on the unhealthy qualities of a Two, and these are the negative qualities to be aware of in romantic relationships. For example, Individualists can become self-focused, overly needy, and have an overwhelming need to help others (especially when they don't want help). If Individualists work on displaying the healthy qualities in a romantic relationship, they can make an amazing partner full of passion and lots of romance.

Lauren, a twenty-something Enneagram Four, is a single woman who lives a very busy, creative lifestyle. Although sometimes she feels like she's too busy to find a romantic partner, there are moments when she wants to experience the passion and romance associated with a relationship. There's one problem though: She has pretty high expectations. This may come from her access line to the Enneagram One, but is also part of the uniqueness of Individualists. She could feel like she can't match up with them. Lauren has gone out on several dates recently, like twenty-somethings do, and was left feeling like none of them really understood who she is, what she does for a living, and other characteristics about herself that are important. Though we don't have an outcome for Lauren's story quite yet, it's important to recognize that Fours want to be understood more than anything. Seek to understand them.

DATING AN ENNEAGRAM FOUR

Special and unique dates are extremely important to Enneagram Fours. In their minds, what is the point of a date if it isn't a special or unique experience? Fours desire dates to be filled with deep and meaningful conversations. This could be intimate conversations in a restaurant that has ambiance, or it could be deep conversations while watching the sun set. Fours also enjoy anything that gives them the ability to be creative. Specific date ideas for Fours could be doing something romantic that you have seen in their favorite movie, or taking them to do pottery or canvas painting as a way to tap into their creative side.

Relationships with Family

Individualists often feel like the black sheep in family relationships. I always think of the song from *Sesame Street* that goes, "One of these things is not like the other." Because they aren't like anyone else, not even other Individualists. Fours have a love–hate relationship with being unlike anyone else. They want to be different and unique, but they also want to be understood by their family members. They live for the connections they have with their family members and value the relationships they have with them. They are pretty good at setting aside intentional time to have deep conversations and moments with family and will often express just how important those moments are to them. Environment is extremely important to Fours, so their homes will be filled with warm and inviting scents, colors, and feelings as a way for their family members to experience that environment, as well.

Tiffany is a wife, daughter, and mother who is an aspiring interior designer. With an eye for design, she is also keen on the way the homes feel when she works with her clients. She is the same exact way with her own home, always having candles lit, lights dimmed, and the most perfect and inviting home decor. Environments for her are all about how others feel in that space, not just if they like how it looks. Tiffany's family knows that environments are important to her, and they do what they can to support that feeling. Even though she keeps her home a certain way because it feels inviting and comfortable to her, she ultimately wants her family to experience the same feelings she does when everyone is together.

Be the Best Four You Can Be

If only we could all have relationships with Fours: I think the world would be a much better place, full of celebrating uniqueness, demonstrating empathy, and being okay with feeling our feelings. I don't know about you, but I want to know Fours and be known by Fours. And that's all they want from us: to be known and understood. To all of the Fours out there, now that you have this information and know how you interact in relationships, it can only get better from here. Focus on the amazing Four that you are and the healthy traits that make you unique, and healthy relationships are sure to come your way.

FIVE TIPS TO BE YOUR BEST SELF IN THE REAL WORLD

1. Sit with your emotions. Feel all of the feelings. Stay there for a little, but don't stay there forever.

2. Be careful about withdrawing when you feel yourself becoming upset by someone's actions or behavior. Try being direct with people instead.

3. Instead of being envious of others, focus on the abilities and traits you have that they do not. Instead of focusing on what you don't have, celebrate the special and unique traits that make you you.

4. Give space to your creative side, whether that is making a career with those skills or being intentional about using those talents.

5. Practice living in the present, instead of reflecting on the past or looking forward to the future. Practice not being envious of others' present moments. Focus on what your own present looks like.

PRACTICAL RELATIONSHIP STRATEGIES FOR AN INDIVIDUALIST

1. Try not to have expectations in a partner that are unrealistic. Yeah, they aren't going to be just like you. But you wouldn't want that anyway.

2. Try not to push your partner away when you're sitting in your emotions. Instead, invite them in and show them what it means to be an empath.

3. Because you're an empath, you're naturally going to be carrying the burdens of your partner. That's what we love about you, Fours, but remember to have someone alongside you as well.

4. It's important to communicate your needs to your partner. At times, you may feel like you don't have any or that you're unable to identify what they would be. However, remember that relationships need to be full of equality.

5. Remember that you are unique, special, and original, so you shouldn't expect people to treat you any differently than that. If they can't see those unique traits, don't be afraid to show them.

Type

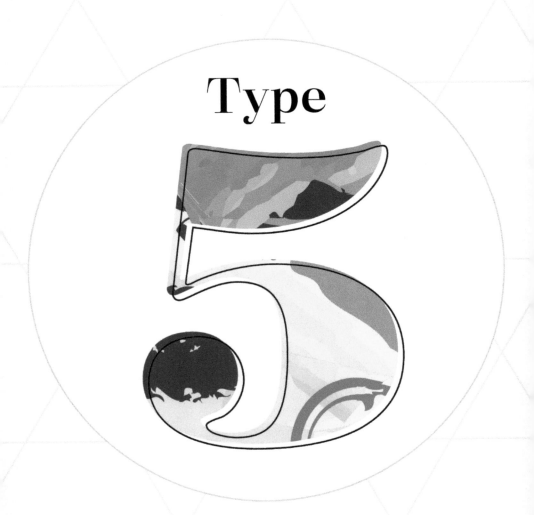

CHAPTER SIX

The Investigator

Enneagram Five. One of the hardest numbers on the Enneagram to understand. Maybe it's because of how quiet they are. Or maybe it's because they just never really tell us who they are and why they do things the way that they do. It's part of what we love about the mysterious Five. Enneagram Fives, also known as *The Investigator,* are motivated by a need to be seen as competent or an intellectual by those around them. When Fives are at their best, they are extremely smart, sensitive, and independent. However, sometimes their stubbornness can get the best of them, causing them to become somewhat of a know-it-all who can be critical of others. Buckle up, Fives. Let's examine how The Investigator interacts in relationships with others.

Getting to Know The Investigator

The Investigator. The Observer. The Intellectual. Lover of knowledge, learning, and capable of accomplishing things. Fives are hard to figure out because they are reserved. Fives are extremely private with every aspect of their lives. It's not necessarily because they don't want to let you in, but because they don't really think it matters. Being around a lot of people tends to drain Fives, so they often keep people out to not experience that type of overwhelm. They have a deep desire to understand every aspect of life and won't stop trying to gain information until they do. Here are some other qualities of an Enneagram Five:

» Fair

» Knowledgeable

» Persevering

» Curious

» Intense

» Researcher

» Thinker

» Subject expert

» Open-minded

» Self-reliant

Common Mistypes

People often mistype as a Five if they are introverted and like to spend time alone. But Fives aren't the only type on the Enneagram that can be considered introverted. The most common mistypes of a Five are Types One, Three, and Nine. Fives and Ones can look similar because they are both intellectual and hardworking. However, Ones are much more attuned to the feelings of others than Fives. Similarly, Fives and Threes seem alike because of their work ethic and how success-oriented they are. The main difference is that Threes are very focused on their outward appearance and how others view them, whereas Fives are not concerned with that at all. Finally, Fives and Nines look similar because they are both private and introverted types and both value personal space. The differences, however, are that Nines will do whatever they have to do to avoid conflict, whereas Fives typically don't mind when conflict exists. Nines also react to things mostly with anger, whereas Fives just retreat into their thoughts.

Childhood

Enneagram Fives as children are usually more withdrawn and isolated than other children. They may feel like they don't relate to other kids because they are interested in different things. These children spend a lot of time reading and gaining knowledge through books. These traits as children teach them how to be independent and rely solely on themselves. Not that they don't rely on their parents, but these children learn the art of being comfortable by themselves. Investigators as children typically excel at school and maintain good grades. They usually don't have huge social groups, but they do focus on meaningful connections with the friends they do have.

Worldview

The Investigators view the world as if resources are scarce. This means they must do whatever they can to conserve their time, energy, and money. Investigators think if they don't conserve these things, then they will be taken away from them. This is partially why Fives are known for keeping to themselves, because they protect their resources. Fives in general are usually pretty conservative with their finances, due to their fear of being depleted in that area, too. It is up to them and only them to maintain all of their resources.

Strengths and Weaknesses

Like the other Enneagram types, Fives have many positive as well as negative traits. Fives are really good at just standing back and observing situations. If you ever forget something happened because you were too busy socializing or focusing on something else, you can guarantee that a Five will remember, because they are usually in the background and paying attention. Another strength of the Investigators is their ability to not succumb to social pressures of who and what they should be. Fives are concerned with what is considered good and right to the world, similar to Ones. They want to be seen as competent and as having good ethics and morals. Fives also never stop investigating a situation until they come to an understanding. If they give you a piece of information, chances are it's probably true. Of course, there are some weaknesses to Fives, mostly around their lack of emotions. It doesn't necessarily mean they don't experience emotions, but they don't know how to accurately identify or display them. Fives struggle in social situations and need ample opportunities to recharge after experiencing them. They also tend to have a "know-it-all" attitude, pushing people away with their defensive demeanor.

Dealing with Conflict

Enneagram Fives typically handle conflict in a rational way. What I mean by this is that they usually spend time collecting their thoughts before responding to the conflict. They think about the best way to approach it and they go from there. They don't necessarily love conflict, but they are always prepared to deal with it.

Enneagram Five Wings

The way that the wings work for Fives is extremely interesting. I just spent a lot of time talking about how Investigators have a difficult time identifying and labeling their feelings. "Feelings" is pretty much a Four's middle name, remember? So, a Five with a strong Four wing is definitely going to be more in tune with their feelings. They will also be more creative, sensitive, and empathetic than traditional Fives. Investigators who lean more on their Six wing will be a little more outgoing and extroverted than other Fives. They also excel at solving problems and resolving issues. However, they could also take on some of the not-so-good Six traits, like worrying and experiencing anxiety.

THREE FAMOUS INVESTIGATORS

Some of the most influential people in the business world (not to mention the wealthiest) are Enneagram Fives.

- Albert Einstein was a stereotypical Investigator, with his vast knowledge and competent skill set. Not only was he known for being intelligent and developing the theory of relativity, Einstein stated that he had a never-ending curiosity.

- Another famous Enneagram Five is Jane Goodall, the world's most well-known expert on chimpanzees. A true Five, Jane has spent almost her entire life researching chimpanzee social and family life, needing to know everything there is to know about them.

- Finally, Bill Gates, founder of Microsoft Corporation, is identified as a Type Five. Bill Gates has always wanted to gain as much information as possible by reading and researching things relevant to his career.

Type
5

Relationships with The Investigator

Relationships with The Investigator can be complicated and full of the other party wondering how the Five is feeling at all times. However, they can also be full of many great qualities that lead to healthy relationships. The three qualities I think of when it comes to Investigators in relationships are mysterious, self-sufficient, and curious. Obviously, there are many more words that could describe any type of relationship with a Five, but these are the three we are going to focus on.

Fives have mysterious ways about them in all aspects of their lives, not just in relationships. This means that sometimes you just might not know what's going on with them, and you have to be okay with it. That's the beauty of the Enneagram, knowing the traits about people whom you interact with and how you can best support them. Investigators often keep their thoughts to themselves and don't display what they are thinking or how they are feeling. This can leave people wondering what is actually going on with them. Some Enneagram types who may have more of an issue with this are those who need validation. The reality is, a Five will not provide that validation in any rela-tionship, no matter the type of relationship it is. Another thing that might lead to Investigators seeming mysterious is their lack of communication. Fives find it difficult to make small talk, for sure, but they also have a hard time communicating in general. Mystery isn't necessarily always a bad thing. Having some level of mystery in relationships keeps things entertaining, as long as it is a healthy amount.

Investigators are extremely independent and have no issue being completely self-reliant. In fact, they don't actually want help from others and get annoyed when they feel smothered. In relationships, Fives are usually doing things for themselves first and others second. It's not necessarily on purpose or to hurt someone's feelings—they just don't really think about it.

They've always taken care of themselves. Fives will want to make sure they can maintain their independence in the relationship, whether it's with a coworker, friend, romantic partner, or family member. They hate feeling like they are being controlled and will often withdraw even more if they feel like it's getting to that point. It's easy to tell if you've crossed their boundaries because they will feel like their independence is being threatened and will pull back from the situation.

Investigators are extremely curious. This comes from their need to gain any and all knowledge and insight. They will be the same way in relationships. They are genuinely curious about who you are and what you bring to the relationship. Whether you're a colleague, friend, family member, or romantic partner, Fives will always want to learn as much as they can about you. They just might do it quietly. Instead of playing Twenty Questions or asking about your favorite color, they will be silently observing to see what they can learn about you. This curiosity is evident outside of their individual relationships as well. They will be curious about the things that you are about; they just have a hard time effectively communicating about it.

Relationships with Colleagues

Work relationships can be weird in general, right? You never know where those boundaries can cross between an actual friendship and strictly coworker relationship. It's especially tricky when you work with someone who is a Five because they are skilled at setting boundaries. If you work with an Investigator, chances are you've been left wondering if you upset them, why they are so quiet, and what is actually going on in their head. Fives will have more boundaries set at work because they excel at focusing on the task at hand. Although it might be tempting to show up at their office or work space to talk about your fantasy draft, just don't. Situations like that make Fives feel like their personal space is being threatened. The best way to interact with

Enneagram Fives at work is to give them their space, respect their boundaries, and accept the fact that group projects might actually be a nightmare to them.

Carl is an Enneagram Five and works in an office setting with some Sevens (The Enthusiasts), some Twos (The Helpers), and a few other Enneagram types. If you know anything about Sevens and Twos, they are pretty outgoing, love conversation, and want to be friends with everyone, which just doesn't fly with Carl. A lot of his coworkers eat lunch together every day, while he will either go out somewhere or eat at his desk alone. People can't understand why he does that, and they feel like he may not enjoy spending time with them. The reality is that it depletes Carl's energy level to spend all of that time with other people. Carl needs those experiences in small doses. Carl actually said that once their company learned about the Enneagram and each other's specific types, people started to understand why he would do the things he does in the work-place. The Sevens and Twos, specifically, no longer think that he's mad at them when he retreats—they just know that he needs to recharge.

Relationships with Friends

Even though many people become friends with others who have shared interests, Fives, especially, do so because it makes the interactions easier for them. Investigators are extremely loyal to their friends, with some friendships spanning multi-ple decades and life experiences. This is because it's easier for Fives to maintain friendships than to pursue new ones. If these friendships didn't exist, they may not end up making new friends because of the likelihood of it being an overwhelming experience for them. When spending time with their friends, Enneagram Fives tend to come out of their shell a little more because they are with people whom they trust and have shared experiences. They feel like these people truly know them and accept them for who they are.

Mark, an Enneagram Five, has a group of friends who all went to high school together. Most of them even went to college together, and that's really where their friendships bloomed because there was a high level of comfort from hanging out with people from his hometown. But what really maintained his friendships was the fact that they all had shared interests, and honestly, they're all kind of similar. They don't mind sitting in silence and watching a sports game, and they talk about things they care about (pretty much the fact that they all like the same sports team or other similar interests). So, here's the lesson in those situations: It's not that Fives can't become friends with any new people or hang out with people who aren't like them; it's that you have to make a conscious effort to get to know them and their interests. That is what will bring them out of their shell, and they will be more comfortable holding conversations around those types of topics. Mark has since realized that he was only hanging out with people whom he has been friends with for a long period of time and has intentionally tried to place himself in situations where he would be forced to meet new people. Is it comfortable? Absolutely not. Is it essential to growth? Absolutely.

Romantic Relationships

Those who are in romantic relationships with a Five will always be kept wondering because of the mysteriousness of Fives. But Investigators have an uncanny ability to allow the intimate relationship to break through the boundaries they have set with other people. Because Fives spend a great deal of time analyzing and investigating relationships before proceeding, they are absolutely sure they want to be with you and make this relationship work. They don't make decisions, especially big ones like relationships, without completely thinking them through.

DATING AN ENNEAGRAM FIVE

It's most likely hard for an Enneagram Five to communicate what they would like a date with them to look like. But let's think about the qualities that we know about Enneagram Fives. They love learning about things and anything that gives them that sense of knowledge that they crave. Fives feel like dates with their partners need to have a purpose, and a purpose to them would be to be able to learn something from them. Specific date ideas for Enneagram Fives would be to go to museums, libraries, exploring different and new cities, as well as experiencing other cultures.

However, they can still sometimes feel like they need time apart from their partner to recharge. Another thing to consider is The Investigator's ability to be self-sufficient. If they have a partner who is constantly wanting to help, this could push them away. A healthy relationship with a Five would look a lot like respecting each other's boundaries and learning to communicate specifically what they need and want from a romantic partner. It takes a lot for Investigators to appear vulnerable, but with the right partner, it can happen.

Janine is an Enneagram Five who is married to an Enneagram Two (The Helper). This relationship combination is always interesting because as we just learned, Fives tend to need space to recharge. Twos, on the other hand, don't really know what personal space is, and they rely on relationships for their fulfillment. This is exactly what was going on in Janine's relationship. She was feeling frustrated because everywhere she looked it felt like her partner was always there. Unsolicited help was pretty much his middle name, after all. Most people would think that his behavior was generous and kind, and to him, it was—but to Janine, it was annoying. Janine feels like she can do everything herself and doesn't need the assistance of her partner for small, mundane tasks. The problem here was that this wasn't being communicated, so they were stuck in an unhealthy pattern. The Two pushes, the Five pulls away. The Two pushes further, and the Five pulls further away. Once this small behavior was identified, Janine and her partner learned that it's a balancing act and that, ultimately, communication is key.

Relationships with Family

In a family setting, Enneagram Fives will most likely be the person who is a walking Google search. What I mean is that they know everything. And I mean everything. If Enneagram Fives are parents, their children can count on them to have an answer for all of the questions they ask. Fives are also usually in the

background of family gatherings and holidays. They are typically silent observers, taking in all of the behaviors and actions
around them. Though they might engage with people with whom
they feel comfortable, they will most likely sit back and wait for
other people to engage them first. These types of encounters
always deplete their energy, and they will be looking for ways
to rest and recharge before the next family event. This can be
confusing to some family members who don't understand the
Enneagram Five's personality. Some might even be offended
or think the Five is strange for being so quiet and reserved.
But it's important for people to seek out The Investigator and
initiate conversations with them, as it will help them feel more
comfortable.

Max is an Enneagram Five who married into a rather large
family. By rather large family, I'm talking 10 total adults (including his in-laws). Not only is this family large in size, but they also
have extremely large personalities, and it is quite overwhelming
for Max. At family functions, Max can usually be found in the
background, observing the wildness of the family, hanging out
with the kids, or just making his presence unknown. And that's
the way he likes it. When there are celebrations like his birthday
and Christmas, he hates being the center of attention and feels
awkward opening gifts in front of people. At first, Max's in-laws
had a difficult time connecting with him, often thinking he didn't
like them or want to spend time with them. It wasn't that at all.
In fact, he really, genuinely enjoys his in-laws. But being with the
extended family absolutely drained him. Now that the family
has the knowledge of the Enneagram, everyone knows that
Max needs his time to recharge, and if he's sitting in a corner
being silent, a gentle nudge will bring him into the fray, if only for
a minute.

Be the Best Five You Can Be

Breathe easy, Fives. I know you don't like the attention on you. But that wasn't so bad, right? The purpose of learning all of these things is so that we can better understand who you are and what you need from us. So, take this information (which I know you love gaining) and put it into action (which I know you love doing). Pretty soon, you will be climbing the ladder of growth. But don't worry, it can be all from the privacy of your own home if that's what you'd like. We all need Fives in our lives, or else we'd never know anything.

FIVE TIPS TO BE YOUR BEST
SELF IN THE REAL WORLD

1. Speak up. It might be hard for you to gather your thoughts and then vocalize them, but it will be helpful to communicate them to others.

2. Practice expressing your feelings. This may need to be something you seek support to help you accomplish. We know your feelings are in there—we just have to work on getting them out.

3. Spend time with people who don't like the same things you do. It will be uncomfortable at first, but it will also be good practice for interacting with others and will help open you up to new people.

4. Realize that it's okay to be quiet. It's totally okay!

5. Learn to trust yourself and your actions more than you already do. This may take some time. Correction: This will take some time. But trusting yourself will move you into the healthy side of your type.

PRACTICAL RELATIONSHIP STRATEGIES FOR AN INVESTIGATOR

1. Learn to identify your own feelings as well as your partner's feelings—what they need, what they want, for example.

2. When you feel a certain way about someone, tell them. And showing them, too, won't hurt.

3. If you feel like someone is crossing your boundaries, communicate with them what those boundaries mean to you and why they are in place.

4. When you are at a family function or on a double date, try not to prove that you know something about everything.

5. Yes, you need to be patient with others, but you also need to be patient with yourself. Real change and growth take time.

Type

CHAPTER SEVEN

The Loyalist

The Loyalist. This type makes up some of the kindest and most generous human beings. Enneagram Sixes can have the reputation of being anxiety-filled human beings who sit at home and worry all day. Wrong. I could honestly write an entire chapter on each of the stereotypes associated with each type. There is so much more to The Loyalist than the fact that they worry sometimes. That is not even one of the main traits associated with them, and I understand why they might get upset when people make assumptions. Enneagram Sixes, also known as *The Loyalist*, are motivated by the need to feel safe and secure, and they fear being without support or guidance. Other names for The Loyalist are *The Loyal Skeptic* and *The Loyal Guardian*. But notice that the word "loyal" is always in the title. Sixes are loyal to people and beliefs. Let's go deeper into these qualities of the Enneagram Six.

Getting to Know The Loyalist

The word *loyal* is defined as "giving or showing firm and constant support or allegiance to a person or institution." Reliable. Responsible. Always prepared. Those are just a few traits that describe Enneagram Sixes and who they are. And not only who they are, but why they do the things that they do. It always goes back to being loyal to a person, cause, or the environment. They tend to have either strong or resistant relationships with authority figures, meaning there's no in-between. They either enjoy those relationships or struggle with adhering to them. Loyalists do struggle with anxiety at times, but it's usually related to when they're feeling unsafe or without security. Loyalists do the things that they do based on what makes them feel safe and secure. Here are some other qualities of a Six:

» Hardworking

» Engaging

» Trustworthy

» Skeptical

» Guarded

» Problem-solver

» Doubtful

» Warm

» Courageous

» Structured

Common Mistypes

People sometimes mistype as an Enneagram Six if they are regularly experiencing some sort of anxiety or worry. But remember, it's not the behavior, and any type can experience anxiety—it's the motivation behind it. Are people feeling anxious specifically due to their need to feel safe and secure? Some common mistypes of Sixes are Types One, Two, and Four. Both Ones and Sixes worry, but Ones worry about making mistakes, whereas Sixes worry about most everything. Ones are also more willing to take risks in life than Sixes. Both Sixes and Twos are warm and inviting to others. The difference is that Twos need acceptance from others, whereas Sixes need certainty. Additionally, Twos typically have more outgoing personalities than

Sixes. Both Fours and Sixes can struggle with self-doubt, but there are key differences. Fours are part of the feeling center and focus their energy on those feelings, whereas Sixes are part of the thinking center and focus more on thinking than their feelings. Another key difference is the way they display their loyalty. Fours are loyal to themselves, before they are loyal to others. Sixes are just the opposite. They are loyal to others first, and to themselves last.

Childhood

Enneagram Sixes as children are often hesitant and careful with every step they take through their childhood. With fear as their guide, they stay safe by not venturing out of their comfort zone. However, these kids are some of the kindest and most likeable children to be around. It can sometimes be difficult for these children to make friends because they are constantly questioning themselves and wondering if they said or did the right thing. As mentioned, Sixes usually have a defining relationship with authority figures. Either they look to authority figures for guidance and protection, or they want to rebel against them. Enneagram Sixes as children can experience heightened anxiety and can be fearful of the smallest of things. This could be because of what they think might be threatening their safety and security, their core desires in life.

Worldview

The Loyalist views the world as a dangerous place. They often feel like things aren't definitive and they have no way of knowing what can and will happen, which is obviously true, but they have a hard time being okay with not knowing. Enneagram Sixes believe that the world is shaky and unknown, but also that they will be able to give it structure, stability, and support, and that they will be safe and secure because of that. The world is scary, but they can make it better.

Type

The Counterphobic Six

Let me introduce you to the Counterphobic Six. Enneagram Sixes are the only type on the Enneagram that actually has two types within one. I know, it sounds rather confusing. The Counterphobic Six has the same motivations and desires as the traditional (also known as *Phobic*) Six, they just act on them differently. Instead of being anxious and afraid, they confront their fears head-on in an assertive and direct way. Counterphobic Sixes can sometimes look a lot like an Enneagram Eight (The Challenger), but the assertiveness is coming from a different place. Counterphobic Sixes confront the fears because that is what makes them feel safe and secure, instead of retreating and being bound by anxiety. That is the biggest and best strength of a Counterphobic Six.

Strengths and Weaknesses

The other strengths of an Enneagram Six are the same for both Counterphobic and Phobic Sixes. They are deeply committed to their loved ones and the people close to them, and others can always count on them to be prepared. Like all types, there are some weaknesses when it comes to The Loyalist. They typically have a difficult time making decisions, not because they don't know what they want the decision to be, but because they aren't confident in their decision-making skills. They also won't be caught dead making a decision until they have all of the information that goes along with it. Sixes can also struggle with self-confidence because it is hard for them to not worry about what they could be doing wrong. Though some types struggle with self-confidence because of what other people think of them, Sixes are worried about how they see themselves.

Dealing with Conflict

Because of an Enneagram Six's relationship with authority, they immediately seek others' opinions when trying to work through and resolve conflict. They trust others more than they trust themselves so they need to seek guidance from authority

THREE FAMOUS LOYALISTS

Three famous people who are known for being Loyalists are Ellen DeGeneres, Princess Diana, and the *Seinfeld* character George Costanza.

- Ellen being an Enneagram Six was surprising to me at first because of her extremely upbeat personality (probably her Seven wing), but I can totally see it now. She is steadfast in her values and passionate about causes. She is extremely playful and wants other people to feel safe and secure, much like herself.

- Similarly, Princess Diana was very altruistic and considered a very influential woman. However, it is publicly known that she had a difficult time trusting those around her, as well as trusting her own decisions. She had been heard saying that her sister was the only person she could truly trust.

- Finally, George Costanza from Seinfeld: a big worrier. George would be considered to be an unhealthy Six because of his sociopath tendencies, like low self-esteem, narcissism, and habitual lying. However, he was extremely loyal to his friends and usually behaved in these ways to maintain that loyalty.

figures. Enneagram Sixes will also carefully spend time preparing for the appropriate way to handle the conflict.

Enneagram Six Wings

The wings of an Enneagram Six can drastically change the way they look. When Sixes lean more toward their Five wing, they tend to be more reserved and internal with their thoughts and feelings. They care more about gaining knowledge to be prepared for situations that could occur. When Sixes lean more toward their Seven wing, they are generally more positive and upbeat, as well as more willing to step outside of their comfort zone. Sixes with a strong Seven wing may be less worried and anxious than other Sixes, and they may enjoy interacting in more of a social setting.

Relationships with The Loyalist

Sixes were made for relationships. At least that is what I always think when I talk to people who are in relationships with Sixes. This is because of their immense—you guessed it—loyalty. They are extremely loyal to any and all relationships that they are in. Friends? They've known them for years. Family members? They spend time with them often. Romantic relationships? They're loyal to their partner and to the relationship itself. Three words I think of when I think about Sixes in relationships are supportive, responsible, and playful.

Even though Enneagram Sixes are called The Loyalist, they have many more qualities to them. Loyalists are known for their unending support of the people in their lives. Whether it be an achievement or success story, an Enneagram Six will be cheering loudly in support of them. I think Sixes are supportive people because they crave that same sort of support in return. You know, the whole "golden rule": Treat others how you want to be treated. But I also believe that Sixes are really good at the "platinum rule": Treat others how they want to be treated. And sometimes that makes all of the difference. Sixes know what nonjudgmental, unending support feels like, and they want to ensure that they are acting that way toward the people who matter in their lives.

I always like to think of the Loyalists as the Boy and Girl Scouts of the Enneagram: They are always prepared for whatever comes their way. Responsibility runs deep in their veins because it makes them feel safe and secure. It's the same in friendships, romantic relationships, family relationships, and even relationships at work. They feel responsible for keeping and maintaining the relationship. This means they put a lot of pressure on themselves within the relationship because for the other person, the responsibility feels nice. But it shouldn't be needed all of the time. Responsibility in relationships for Enneagram Sixes looks like taking care of their partner by making sure they have what they need, ensuring their emotions are attended to, and helping them with their own daily responsibilities. Responsibility is extremely important to Sixes.

One thing people don't always realize about Sixes is their level of playfulness. Loyalists can be extremely funny, often without trying to be. Some people have this idea that Sixes are serious all of the time because of their tendency to worry or struggle with anxiety, but the playfulness is often used to mask those struggles. There might be a serious situation going on, but Sixes can use that playful side of them to lighten the mood. In relationships, specifically, they want others to also feel safe and secure with them, and they will use jokes and silliness to become closer to them. However, they are typically only silly with the people they feel most connected to, as it can make them feel vulnerable to show that side of themselves. If you are in a friendship or romantic relationship with a Six who is playful, you know they feel comfortable with you.

Relationships with Colleagues

Similar to relationships in general, Enneagram Sixes are extremely loyal to the people with whom they work. They almost create a sort of bond in the workplace, and their colleagues will always know that they are there for them. However, Sixes do set boundaries, and they will often keep their work friends at work—for protection, of course. This loyalty doesn't stop a Six from feeling inadequate and unconfident at work, which could leak into their relationships with their colleagues. Loyalists also can strongly connect with those who are like-minded in relation to work ethic. For example, Loyalists will want to make sure their colleagues are also showing up on time, working the hours they are supposed to, and not taking too long of a lunch break. Where Ones follow rules to be "good," Sixes enjoy rules and guidelines because it makes them feel secure and shows loyalty to the company and their colleagues.

Jim is an Enneagram Six and works with colleagues who are a variety of types, including Twos, Sevens, and Eights. He often appreciates what they bring to the team, specifically the ability to generate ideas, helpfulness, and charisma. However, Jim's coworkers often expect things of him that he's just not able to provide. Jim's team will be up next to pitch an idea to their boss, and he won't be caught dead being the one to speak. Coming up with the plan or strategy? Definitely. Public speaking? Hard pass. Similarly, when they go to young-professional mixer events, Jim usually sits by himself at a table while his colleagues float around the room, networking and collecting potential customers. Jim's coworkers don't understand this behavior because he seems so sociable with them in the office, but that's because he feels comfortable and secure around them. If they understood this about Jim, it would help him come out of his comfort zone a little more and be more confident in his abilities.

Relationships with Friends

Enneagram Sixes make fantastic friends because they are the most loyal type on the Enneagram. Loyalists are the epitome of a friend. Once they meet and become friends with you, there is no letting go. Loyalists are known for being friends with people for a long time, most of the time from childhood. This is because their best friendships are ones that make them feel safe and secure, and passing time can do that for them. If you're friends with an Enneagram Six, just know that they need your constant support and security. Make sure you're as loyal to them as they are to you. Know that they wouldn't be in your life if you weren't extremely important to them, and they also want that same kind of respect.

Megan (a One) and Carly (a Six) met in college and have been friends for many years. Their friendship consists of shared interests and hobbies, a similar need to plan for things, and a loyalty to each other. The biggest difference, though, is Carly's need to feel secure in the friendship. Although Megan definitely appreciates the security Carly brings to her life, it isn't so much of a necessity for her the way it is for Carly. Another significant difference in their friendship is the reason behind their planning and preparedness. Carly is always thinking about worst-case scenarios: what could go wrong, what she will forget, if bad weather is coming. Megan likes to be prepared because it's what feels right and correct in her world. In friendships, Sixes can teach Ones how to be a little bit more playful and relaxed, while the One can teach the Six consistency and confidence in their decisions.

Romantic Relationships

Loyalists can be amazing partners because of their warm and playful disposition. We already know how important being loyal is to an Enneagram Six, and that's no different in romantic

DATING AN
ENNEAGRAM SIX

Enneagram Sixes really enjoy going on dates with their partners because of the importance of relationships in their lives. However, it's important that they feel comfortable and safe on every date that they are on. This means that surprises usually aren't welcome for Enneagram Sixes. They enjoy when you plan things, but that you tell them about it first. Sixes appreciate things that are meaningful with thought and effort put into it. They also enjoy repeat places, restaurants, and things that they've done before because that is comfortable to them.

relationships. This can be great when they are in a healthy and rewarding relationship. But it can also be problematic when they are in a toxic relationship and have a difficult time leaving because of their deep-seated need to remain loyal. Sixes in relationships often bring their own set of values and what they are passionate about, and they want to share that with their partner. At their best in romantic relationships, Loyalists are supportive, honest, reliable, and committed. However, sometimes their worry and anxiety can creep in and cause issues in a romantic relationship. At their worst in a relationship, Loyalists can be stubborn, sarcastic, and adopt a "my way or the highway" type of mentality. Generally speaking, though, Loyalists are steadfast partners with friendly personalities.

Danny (a Six) and Andrea (a Seven) have been together for many years, but were only introduced to the Enneagram a few years ago. Andrea always says that she wishes that she had known about it earlier on in their relationship because of the benefits she's witnessed over the past few years. As a Seven, Andrea has always been interested in living a big and loud life (we'll talk more about that in the next chapter) and she couldn't understand why her husband was rarely on board with her wild ideas and adventures. After learning the Enneagram, Danny was able to better articulate the parts of him that explained his hesitancy and fear of the unknown. Andrea learned she had to give him space at times to evaluate situations, to help him learn to be confident in his decision-making, and to make sure he knew exactly what he was getting into before they went on their adventures. It's not that he wouldn't go, but he needed to know all of the possibilities. One thing Andrea always knew about Danny, however, was that he would always be there to show her love and support her endeavors.

Relationships with Family

You can spot a Loyalist in a family structure because they are almost always worrying the most. It may not always be an outward type of worry, and they may worry about things without even talking about them. When Sixes are parents, that worry can lead to difficulty allowing their children to explore on their own. In family relationships, Sixes also have a difficult time setting boundaries because of their inability to speak up when they feel uncomfortable. However, people will love that their Enneagram Six family member is extremely prepared for anything they might encounter. The Loyalist will be the one to make a dinner reservation, remember to pack all SPFs of sunscreen, double- and triple-check if they've remembered the tickets, and have Advil on hand. Always prepared, always willing, always loyal— that's an Enneagram Six.

Laura's dad is an Enneagram Six, and she was recounting to me what that looked like for her growing up. The first thing she said to me was that he was always prepared. Have a stomachache? Here, take some Pepto-Bismol tablets. Heartburn? Here, have some Tums. It started raining? Here, you can have my umbrella. Getting bitten by mosquitos? Here's some bug spray and anti-itch cream. Another thing she recalled from her childhood was her dad's love of routine because of his need for familiarity. Every summer, they went on vacation to the beach and rented the same house. Same beach, same house, same comfort level. Every year for his birthday, he wanted to go to the same restaurant. Same coffee order at the local Starbucks. Same car, just different colors over the years. But what Laura also said was that her dad was always there for her, and she never had to wonder about it. He was always supportive of her goals and desires. He was always extremely nurturing and cared deeply about his children. And he made them laugh like no other.

Be the Best Six You Can Be

It's difficult to spend an entire chapter thinking about ourselves, especially for Sixes, as they don't want to spend more time in their head than they already have to. But that wasn't so bad, right? The more you know about yourself, the more you can work to adjust some of those not-so-healthy qualities you may find yourself gravitating toward. The good news is that you're in control of changing those behaviors and can make those changes at a pace that feels comfortable. You know, Loyalists' biggest need—comfort.

FIVE TIPS TO BE YOUR BEST SELF IN THE REAL WORLD

1. Practice mantras. You know, that positive self-talk that makes you uncomfortable? It's like going to the gym for your brain. If you say enough positive things about yourself, you'll start to believe them and will be able to combat some of that fear or worry.

2. Remember that it's okay to have fears and worries. Try not to feel guilty for having and experiencing them. Give yourself permission to experience those feelings.

3. When you're feeling anxious, try to get to the root of the issue. Why are you feeling this way? When was the last time you felt this way? What can you do moving forward so you don't feel this way again?

4. Physical activity is going to do wonders for your type specifically. It will help make sure that you're staying out of your head and focusing on the activity.

5. Divide tasks into to-do lists. It may help keep you from feeling overwhelmed.

PRACTICAL RELATIONSHIP STRATEGIES FOR A LOYALIST

1. Work on being patient with others. They may not be as hard of a worker as you. They may not be as prepared as you. But they are trying their best.

2. Try to remember that your stress levels can affect those around you. When feeling stressed, recognize the behavior and figure out how to remedy it.

3. Communicate how you are feeling about something. You may feel the need to keep it inside, but people need to know how you're feeling to better understand you.

4. Set clear boundaries with those whom you are in relationships. This will help you not feel drained or overwhelmed by their needs.

5. Don't be afraid to take a risk, even if it seems scary. It might feel out of your comfort zone to get together with that friend or go on a date, but good things come from spending time in that uncomfortable place.

Type

CHAPTER EIGHT

The Enthusiast

Enneagram Seven. The most enthusiastic and optimistic type on the Enneagram. The king or queen of the optimistic triad. The glass isn't just half full, it's completely full and overflowing. Enneagram Seven, also known as *The Enthusiast,* cannot get enough out of life. They constantly need more. Sevens are motivated by a need to always move on to the next best thing. Their greatest desire is to always have their needs fulfilled, and their biggest fear is experiencing negative emotions and boredom. When Sevens are at their best, they are fulfilled and content right where they are, and they can rest without having to keep "doing." Let's talk more about the amazing characteristics of an Enneagram Seven.

Getting to Know The Enthusiast

Enthusiast is defined as "a person who is highly interested in a particular activity or subject." This makes me laugh because Enneagram Sevens are highly interested in life itself. Sure, maybe they are interested in one thing. But that's only until they get bored by it and move to the next exciting thing in their life. Enthusiasts are also known as being everyone's cheerleader in life. They absolutely hate negative experiences and can sometimes cover them up to not deal with the painful feelings associated with them. Because of their inability to sit with negative experiences, they tend to have a difficult time working through them and can experience negative consequences of that moving forward. Overall, Sevens are optimistic, carefree people with a desire to do all of the things. Here are some other qualities of a Seven:

» Spontaneous

» Positive

» Upbeat

» Adventurous

» Flexible

» Encouraging

» Playful

» Scattered

» Practical

» Impatient

» Optimistic

» Impulsive

» Generous

Common Mistypes

People can mistype as a Seven when they consider themselves to be positive and outgoing people who are "high on life." Many other types also have some of those personality characteristics. Some common mistypes for Sevens are Types Two, Three, and Nine. Sevens and Twos look similar because they are both typically optimistic and outgoing. However, there are key differences: Twos focus on others' needs first, whereas Sevens focus on what they need (which is usually a new adventure). Another difference is that Twos fear being disliked most of all, whereas Sevens fear that they are missing out on something. Threes and Sevens seem similar because they both have a lot of energy, but Threes are more efficient and purposeful, whereas Sevens go with the flow. Sevens and Nines seem similar because they both generally avoid conflict and wish for life to be enjoyable. However, Nines are typically more slow-moving than Sevens. Additionally, Nines enjoy slowing down to enjoy the ride, whereas Sevens are focused on what is next.

Childhood

Enneagram Sevens in childhood are always on the go and on to the next sporting event or activity. And here's the thing: They love it! Their parents don't have to talk them into doing anything because they already want to do it without needing a gentle nudge. Enneagram Sevens are always the children who entertain others—think the class clown. They thrive off attention for whatever they do. Enthusiasts as children also struggle with boredom and can often be seen spending their summers complaining that they are bored because they need to be stimulated with activities regularly. Enneagram Seven children also feel personally responsible for other kids having a good time whenever they are around. This gets them in trouble at times when they want to show people a good time no matter the path it takes to get there.

Worldview

The Enthusiasts view the world as if it is empty and they are responsible for filling it up. They feel as if there aren't enough possibilities and experiences in the world and they are solely responsible for generating all of the fun and exciting things that the world could possibly have. Sevens also view the world as if it is automatically a negative place and it is their job to bring happiness and joy into it. Sevens sometimes believe the world will remain negative and boring unless they do something about it.

Strengths and Weaknesses

Even though Enneagram Seven is called The Enthusiast, that does not mean that these types are always upbeat and only full of positive qualities. Just like other types, Enthusiasts have many strengths and weaknesses when it comes to the ins and outs of who they are. The most obvious strength of a Seven is their ability to turn any negative experience into a positive one. However, this can also serve as a weakness if they aren't appropriately working through their pain. Another strength is their carefree way of living, which often leads them to meeting new people, experiencing different things, and an ability to always go with the flow. They are also exceptional cheerleaders for the people in their lives, which we will talk more about later. Sevens can get into trouble when they have to always be on the go and experiencing something new. Sometimes they can seem scattered because they're always thinking about the next thing. Because of this, Sevens can have a hard time finishing the things they start. They have amazing ideas, but they struggle with follow-through because they just want to move on to the next idea.

Dealing with Conflict

Enneagram Sevens also want everyone to like them so they have a hard time addressing conflict with people whom they love. Most of the time Sevens will use humor and joking around while they are resolving conflict to take the pressure off of the seriousness of the issue. This is to quickly resolve the conflict and move on to having fun.

Enneagram Seven Wings

The wings always change the way that Enneagram types look, but it's even more apparent with The Enthusiast. Here's why: A Seven with a stronger Six wing might be a little bit more hesitant than traditional Sevens. Instead of the glass always being full, those with more access to the Six wing might tap into that half-empty mentality every now and then because they are more

THREE FAMOUS ENTHUSIASTS

You can probably think of famous Enthusiasts because of their outgoing personalities. The three famous Enthusiasts I always think of are Jim Carrey, Amelia Earhart, and Katy Perry.

- Jim Carrey is an actor and comedian with the most energy of any actor I've ever seen. Known for his impressions, it's no surprise he's an Enneagram Seven.

- Amelia Earhart was known for being curious for adventure from a young age. She was the first female pilot to attempt to fly solo across the Atlantic Ocean for crying out loud! Talk about adventure. A true Seven.

- Katy Perry is a singer and songwriter known for her electric personality and eccentric outfits. She lives life out loud and has her music to show for it.

aware of things that could go wrong or worries that may come to fruition. Alternately, a Seven with a stronger Eight wing is likely going to be more assertive than a typical Seven. They have the ability to be extremely powerful people because of their direct and decisive personality. These Sevens are also much better at following through on ideas.

Relationships with The Enthusiast

There will never be a dull moment when you are friends, partners, or part of a family with an Enneagram Seven. Relationships with The Enthusiast will be adventurous and full of optimism and positivity. Forget about ever having a bad day—they definitely won't let that happen. When I think of three words that define Enthusiasts in relationships, they are outgoing, generous, and resilient. Let's talk more about this.

It's probably no surprise to you that Enneagram Sevens are considered outgoing. They are the most extroverted type on the Enneagram and willing to start a conversation with just about anyone. That's no different in relationships. At the beginning of your relationship with them, they will most likely be seeking you out. There will be no shortage of conversation when you are together, and not just with the two of you but with the server at a restaurant, the cashier at a store, and a person just walking along the street. They are always willing to put themselves out there to generate conversation and to ultimately meet new people. Need more friends? Hang out with a Seven. They are sure to introduce you to more people than you could ever imagine. And they know how to pick them.

Enthusiasts are also extremely generous. Sometimes Sevens can look like Twos in this way, because they are always willing to help out others. But the motivation behind the helping is different. For Twos, they help others because it makes them feel needed. Sevens offer help because it's another adventure and they love doing it. Sevens are the friend you call at midnight because your car battery died. Sevens are the people you call after a breakup because you know they will bring joy to your life. Sevens are also generous in the way they want to share their life experiences with you. Sure, they are completely fine and comfortable going to do things by themselves, but they want to share the moment with you because of what you would get out of it, not them. Enthusiasts are just all-around generous humans.

Enthusiasts are also resilient. Now, that might seem like an interesting choice, but let me explain. What I mean by "resilient" is that they are always able to pull themselves back up by the boot-straps if they encounter anything difficult. Part of it could be their Six wing (The Loyalist); Sevens are always ready to make things better in relationships because they are fiercely loyal to their friends and family because their happiness is just as important to a Seven as their own. This also means that if Enthusiasts are ever hurt by someone they love, they will be resilient and not let it deter them from deepening their friendships or relationships with other people. Because let's be honest: Sevens were not made to stay sad. And they won't let you stay sad, either.

Relationships with Colleagues

Enneagram Sevens want to be friends with everyone—that's a fact. It's no different for work relationships with an Enthusiast. They most likely enjoy being friends with their coworkers inside and outside of the workplace. They are the colleague who remembers every birthday and lives to celebrate everyone and anyone. The Enthusiast is the colleague you want to call when you're having a bad or stressful day because you know they will cheer you up and turn things in a positive direction. They are also exceptional at handling emergencies and know just what to do. What you can offer a colleague who is a Seven is a well-thought-out plan because they tend to be scattered, espe-cially with work assignments.

Type
7

Carly, an Enneagram Two, used to work with an Enneagram Seven named Lindsey. Lindsey was the Seven of all Sevens. The queen of the Enthusiasts. The optimist of the optimists. Basically, the ultimate Enneagram Seven. In a lot of ways, they were similar. They both enjoyed helping their colleagues. They were (usually) the bright spot in others' days. They were both full of life. However, there were some clear differences between the two. Lindsey could spend any amount of time with people and would love every second of it. Her entire day was filled with meetings, activities, and get-togethers, and that's exactly how she wanted it. According to Carly, you could often hear Lindsey coming from a mile away, and people remembered her infectious laughter, big personality, and inability to hide her excitement whenever she saw other colleagues. However, Carly was a little bit more reserved, focusing less on the experience of being with people and more concerned about their needs. Carly said that even throughout their stressful jobs, she always knew that she could count on Lindsey to brighten the day because of her optimistic outlook on life.

Relationships with Friends

Enthusiasts make excellent friends because they are always ready for an adventure. No matter the day, no matter the time, you can always count on them for fun. If someone breaks your heart, The Enthusiast will create an elaborate plan to take your mind off them. Want to go to a concert of a band they have never heard of? They're down to go just for the mere thought of experiencing something new. Want to try a new restaurant in town? Absolutely, they are ready for that. However, Sevens do have a hard time with negative feelings and feelings of sadness. It's not necessarily that they will avoid conflict altogether (like Nines), but they have a hard time communicating things that upset them because of their fear of being trapped in emotional pain, so they often just ignore negative feelings completely. As a friend of a Seven, it's important for you to learn to identify the ways they are struggling with this, and assure them that even though it may be painful now, they aren't going to stay there.

Nicole and Chelsey's friendship goes back many years to their high school days. Although they were very different in high school, they had shared interests and a similar friend group. Nicole is an Enneagram Seven, and Chelsey is an Enneagram Six. Chelsey never understood how Nicole could just keep going and going, always wanting to jump from one activity to another. Chelsey said that one time Nicole planned for them to visit a zoo, an amusement park, and finish the day by shopping—all in one day! They got into an altercation because Chelsey felt like she couldn't handle that many activities, and Nicole couldn't understand the issue. Friendships with Sevens need to be balanced. Not everyone is going to want every day to be an adventure (unless they are Sevens themselves). Be mindful of this while in friendships, both new and old.

Romantic Relationships

When Sevens are at an unhealthy place with their Enneagram type, they have a hard time with romantic relationships. This is because unhealthy Sevens have a fear of commitment, a fear of being tied down, a fear of staying in one place. Let's call it what it is: an extreme fear of boredom. However, when they are in a healthy place with their type, they can make excellent partners who are caring, generous, and full of fun times and corny jokes. They like to keep things positive, and they will always be there for you as a support system to make you laugh and look on the bright side of things. Things need to be kept exciting when you are in a romantic relationship with a Seven, as they are not the type to sit on the couch and watch Netflix every night. They want to stay busy with activities and adventures, and they want you to be involved with them as their partner.

DATING AN ENNEAGRAM SEVEN

Enneagram Sevens were created for dates. And not just going out to a restaurant for dinner (although they'd appreciate anything), I'm talking about truly adventurous dates. We know that Enneagram Sevens live for excitement, and it's the same way when going on dates with their partners. They also love surprises, and would love nothing more than for you to plan something that completely blows them away. Specific date ideas for Enneagram Sevens would be anything that keeps them on their toes. Specifically, you will be safe with go-karts, miniature golfing, trivia, axe throwing, dessert or bar hopping, or anything adventurous.

Brandon (Enneagram Seven) and Morgan (Enneagram Five) have been married for a few years. On the surface, it may seem like they are extremely different, but Sevens take on healthy qualities of a Five when they are in a good spot within their type. The biggest difference, of course, is that Morgan is pretty reserved, whereas Brandon is very outgoing. This makes for interesting social gatherings, as Brandon wants to go to everything: family events, mixers, community socials, weddings, you name it. Morgan, however, is exhausted just thinking about those things. Growing up in a large family, she learned to keep to herself and things that felt familiar. Brandon was the complete opposite and felt like he needed to do it all or he would be missing out. The amazing part about this relationship is how they can balance each other out. Morgan teaches Brandon when he needs to take it down a notch and be present, while Brandon introduces Morgan to new activities and adventures. Communication and understanding are key.

Relationships with Family

Is there such a thing as the "family clown?" If so, it would be an Enneagram Seven—full of life, possibilities, and an uncanny ability to make their family members laugh at all times. When I think of Enneagram Sevens in a family structure, they always have great ideas, but struggle to follow through. They want their room to look a certain way, but it ends up being a scattered mess. They procrastinate, but only because they have better things to do. Teenagers are never home in general, but throw in an Enneagram Seven teenager, and you'll think they flew the coop early. They are always getting invited places, always wanting to go out, and making sure they don't miss out on anything. Similar to other relationships, Sevens are always full of positivity in family relationships. Things rarely get them down, and they bring that type of energy to their family members. Life is one big party, and everyone's invited.

Type 7

Michelle (Enneagram One) grew up with Enneagram Sevens, her mom and sister. Talk about a lot of energy in that household! Her sister was younger, but not by much, and she and Michelle were always close. A healthy Enneagram One would have no problem taking on the positive qualities of a Seven, but that's not Michelle's natural way of being. Her mom and sister often butted heads because of their similar personalities. But Michelle would come in the middle and determine right from wrong and make sure it was a fair fight (you know, all Enneagram One traits). The biggest thing Michelle recalled about her life with a Seven mom and sister is that they were always up for an adventure, big or small. Their household was full of laughter. The tears didn't last very long, and the love they all had for each other was positive and uplifting.

Be the Best Seven You Can Be

Sevens are so loved, so fun, and so needed by everyone. That is why we need you at your best. Be the fun-loving, caring, and generous person you are. Crack jokes. Make people laugh. And teach everyone that life really is a party to be embraced. Take breaks when you need to. Be okay with silence sometimes. Remember that even the Energizer Bunny does eventually run out of battery power, and we don't want that to happen to you. You're amazing, and the world needs your joy.

FIVE TIPS TO BE YOUR BEST SELF IN THE REAL WORLD

1. Try to focus on the here and now instead of the future. Focus on what you have, not what you want.

2. Try not to cover up your pain and negative emotions. Reach out to a friend or a trained professional to help you walk through those emotions.

3. Be aware that not everyone is as energetic and fast-paced as you are—and be okay with knowing that.

4. Adjust your impulsiveness. Pause before you act on your desire to be impulsive with your actions and behaviors.

5. Learn to be comfortable in silence. Yes, this might force you to listen to your thoughts. But it may also help for you to work through the silence and into a period of growth.

PRACTICAL RELATIONSHIP STRATEGIES FOR AN ENTHUSIAST

1. Listen to your partner when they are speaking. I mean really listen. Try to shut off your mind from thinking about what is next or what you'll say next.

2. Communicate with your partner about which activities you expect them to attend and at which you're okay to fly solo.

3. Communicate your wants and needs with your partner. And make sure it's not just you communicating with them—listen to what your partner needs from you, too.

4. Be intentional about spending time with your partner. Do things they want to do.

5. Practice pausing before automatically trying to cheer someone up. This is especially important if your partner is an Enneagram Four or Five, as they may need time to process before responding to your energy.

Type

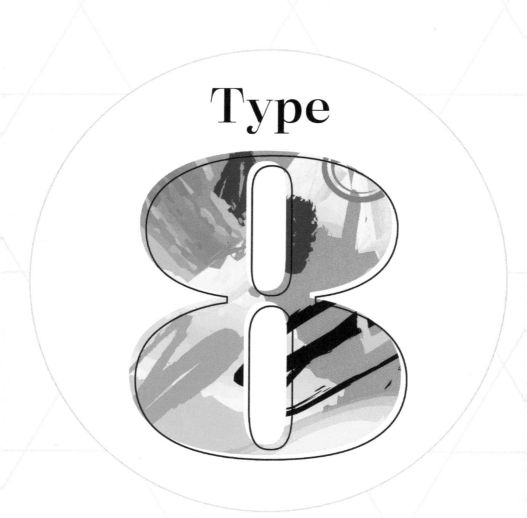

CHAPTER NINE

The Challenger

O h, Enneagram Eight. I hope that I do this chapter justice for you. Eights are amazing humans, full of protection, strength, and confidence. Enneagram Eights get a bad reputation because they can be tough. But usually it's only tough on the outside. Enneagram Eight, also known as *The Challenger*, is motivated by a desire to protect themselves and the environment around them. Their biggest fear is being controlled by others. This is because they are fiercely independent and the captains of their own ships. When Eights are at their best, they are loyal, confident, hardworking, and energetic. Let's do a deep dive into what makes an Enneagram Eight tick.

Type 8

Getting to Know The Challenger

A *challenger* is defined as "a person who disputes the truth of or places themselves in opposition to something," and I can totally see why this name was given to Enneagram Eights. However, I would change this definition to a person who "disputes *to get to* the truth." Eights want to be able to prove their strength, and they fight for what they believe in. Similar to Ones, they are huge protectors of the underdog and often are known for speaking up for others when they feel like others can't do it for themselves. When Eights are at their best, they can be heroic and seen as mentors. However, at their worst, they can be angry, controlling, and harsh at times. Deep down there is a softer side to Eights; they just don't always allow you to see it because of their fear of vulnerability. Here are some more words to describe an Eight:

» Confident

» Protective

» Leader

» Passionate

» Decisive

» Truthful

» Inspiring

» Assertive

» Independent

» Bossy

» Productive

Common Mistypes

People can often mistype as an Eight if they consider themselves to be assertive and determined. However, other types also have those personalities. Some of the common mistypes of an Enneagram Eight are Types One and Three. Eights and Ones are similar because they both consider themselves protectors, and they both fight injustices. However, Ones tend to suppress their opinions, whereas Eights are typically very direct and opinionated. Additionally, Ones don't have the same resistance to vulnerability that Eights do. Eights and Threes are similar because they are both usually assertive and like to take charge in situations. The difference here, though, is that Threes don't love confrontation, whereas Eights feel like it is necessary. Threes are also generally more concerned with their own goals, whereas Eights are more concerned with justice for others.

Childhood

Enneagram Eights during their childhood always feel like they need to protect themselves and others. They often have a lot of energy and big personalities. You can feel their sort of energy when you are around them, even at a young age. Eight children feel like they don't have anyone to stand up for them or do things the way they want them to be done, so they learn to do it on their own. Enneagram Eights challenge their parents on everything they say and do. Don't be surprised if there is a parent–child conflict occurring at multiple stages through-out their lives. Eight children mostly keep their feelings to themselves and act like they can handle anything that comes their way.

Worldview

Eights view the world as if there are two types of people: the powerful and the weak. Eights feel that powerful people will always take advantage of the weak, and that it is their respon-sibility to do something about it. The irony here is that some individuals might consider Eights "powerful people," but the dif-ference is that they feel like they are part of the group working to change the power structure.

Strengths and Weaknesses

Like all types, Challengers have many strengths and weak-nesses when it comes to their Enneagram type. Eights are great protectors. They stick up for the underdog, the weak, and the vulnerable. They also encourage and empower those people to stick up for themselves. Another strength is that Eights are fiercely independent. They are true to who they are, and what you see is what you get. Because of their ability to always be straightforward, you'll never wonder where you stand with them. Often, the straightforward trait can also be seen as a weakness because some people don't know how to handle it. Some people are intimidated by Eights because of their bluntness and willingness to speak their mind. Another weakness of Challengers is their impatience. They have a need to be in control, and if that isn't happening, they can seem extremely impatient. When Eights are at their most unhealthy state, they can be self-centered and insensitive toward others around them.

Dealing with Conflict

Enneagram Eights don't shy away from conflict at all. In fact, they typically embrace it. They see conflict as a way of life and something that needs to be dealt with, typically in a timely manner. They are direct with their words and behaviors and know what they need to do to move on.

Enneagram Eight Wings

The wings of Enneagram Eight are interesting because they can be so different. An Eight with more access to the Seven wing is a little bit more outgoing than the traditional Eight. They tend to be driven by excitement and adventure and are always looking for new activities. An Eight with a stronger Nine wing is a little more laid-back than traditional Eights. They are calmer and have less of a need to always be right. This is because of the Nine's ability to always see multiple sides of a situation.

Relationships with The Challenger

Relationships with Enneagram Eights can be extremely intense one minute, and then the next minute, they are bending over backward to make sure you have what you need. They often feel as if they are solely responsible for ensuring the relationship

THREE FAMOUS CHALLENGERS

When I think about famous people who are Enneagram Eights, I always think about those who are driven to seek justice and stand up for the underdog. Three famous Challengers are Martin Luther King Jr., Serena Williams, and Alecia Beth Moore, the singer also known as Pink.

- I think it's no surprise that Martin Luther King Jr. is an Enneagram Eight because of his activism, specifically being the leader of the civil rights movement. He devoted his life to fighting for civil rights in a nonviolent way. I'd be willing to bet he had strong Seven and Nine wings.

- Serena Williams, a professional American tennis player, also considers herself an activist when she's not dominating on the court. Known for never caring about others' opinions of her, she also devotes herself to activism for black communities and equality.

- Alecia Beth Moore, the singer also known as Pink, is also a Type Eight. Pink is known for constantly pushing boundaries and doing what she wants in her musical career. She also makes it known that she will do her own thing through different looks throughout the years, and that what you see is what you get with her.

is successful. They believe the best relationships are those filled with mutual respect and understanding, and this goes for all types of relationships—friendships, work relationships, romantic relationships, and family relationships. When I think of words to describe any type of relationship with Eights, these three come to mind: committed, independent, and passionate.

Commitment is pretty much an Eight's middle name. They live and breathe commitment. Break a previously planned commitment with them? There's going to be an issue, and you're going to hear about it. On the other hand, people who are in any kind of relationship with Eights will know wholeheartedly that they will never break commitments, and if they say they are going to do something, they will follow through. This commitment is the same for the obligations and events within a relationship, and with the relationship itself. Remember that responsibility they feel to make sure that the relationship is successful? This is because they are committed to the success of the relationship and the individuals who are in it. Commitment is a huge part of relationships with a Challenger.

Another characteristic always prevalent in relationships with Challengers is their need for independence. Sure, they love being with you and spending time together, but they value their independence, meaning they will never be dependent on you for their happiness. Although your friendship or relationship is important to them, they will never depend on it. Additionally, they fully understand that it's great to spend time together, but they also need to spend time apart. Challengers will also not let their opinions or ideas be swayed by those around them. They value others' opinions, but those opinions won't affect them because of the value they put on their own independence and their need to be in control of themselves.

Passion. Intensity. Fire. These are all ways to describe what fuels Enneagram Eights. When they care about you, you'll know. When they're angry with you, you'll know. When you're not sure how they're feeling, well, that will never happen because it will be pretty obvious. Challengers are fueled by passion. Being passionate is defined as "showing or caused by strong feelings or a strong belief." When you are in any kind of relationship with an Eight, they will display passion because of their belief in that relationship. This passion may be shown in the raising of their voice, even though they don't intend to do that. This passion could also be displayed by being a big cheerleader and protector and believing in you as a person. Eights are passionate about helping you be the best version of yourself and showing you how to stand up for yourself and what you need in life.

Relationships with Colleagues

Eights are natural leaders in the workplace because of their ability to conquer tasks and delegate like no other. This may be seen as intimidating or maybe even annoying by the colleagues who work with them, but it is one of the reasons the Enneagram is so important, as it helps us understand each other. Challengers are definitely the colleagues you want to have, because they are always committed to completing tasks in a timely manner. The same commitment and passion they have for other things is transferred to the workplace. Because of their intensity, however, sometimes they can be off-putting to their colleagues if they don't know how to communicate with them.

I spoke with my friend, Amy, who is going to be the supervisor of her department. Amy told me about her new colleague Jennifer. At the first staff meeting, Jennifer spoke about the Enneagram and told everyone that she's an Eight and that sometimes people won't like her but she's okay with that. Amy is an Enneagram Four and is typically sensitive to how others view her. Jennifer proceeded to take over the meeting and assigned tasks to everyone for the week, something that was never done previously (the team actually enjoyed the structure; it was just something new). Amy said that had she not known about the Enneagram, and Enneagram Eight specifically, she

would have felt extremely intimidated by Jennifer and the role she was going to play on their team. They are now able to get along and understand each other better because they have the knowledge of the strengths and weaknesses of each other's Enneagram types.

Relationships with Friends

Challengers are the type of friends you want when you don't know how to stick up for yourself. As protectors, they will make sure no one is saying anything negative about you behind your back. And if someone does, Eights will put them in their place. What you see is what you get with them, and you'll never have to wonder how they feel about you and your friendship with them. If they have an issue with something you're doing or a decision you made, they will argue their opinion to get you to see their side of it. This is because they feel like they would be doing a disservice to the friendship by not being honest, even if it puts the friendship in jeopardy. Challengers are strong in their principles and feel that everyone else should be that way as well.

Bethany (Enneagram Eight) and Briana (Enneagram Six) have been best friends for almost two decades. Their friendship has expanded through college and well into their adult lives. Recently, though, that best friend status has changed because of an incident between them. Briana is in a relationship Bethany doesn't agree with because she feels that Briana deserves better and should be treated with more respect. Because Bethany is an Eight, it's extremely hard for her to sit by and see her friend being treated poorly. She has strong values and beliefs about the way Briana is being treated. Bethany was assertive in stating her opinion but has since given Briana space for her to figure it out. That is a very Enneagram Eight thing to do, as once their piece is shared, they are not going to keep sharing it. It's out there for the person to do with it as they please.

Romantic Relationships

As you now know, Challengers are full of passion when they are in relationships and especially when they are in romantic relationships. They have no problem expressing their wants and desires in romantic relationships, and they wish their partners would do the same. They have extremely high expectations and will not settle on a partner unless someone meets their expectations. Additionally, they value independence in romantic relationships because they strongly believe that who they are is not defined by the relationship they are in. This means they will always encourage their partner to have their own activities, hobbies, and friendships outside of their relationship. Because of Eight's desire to be in control, they like to call the shots and have a hard time being told what to do. Eights love to encourage and empower their partners to be the best person they can be.

Jeff (Enneagram Eight) and Christine (Enneagram Nine) have been married for more than 10 years and have three children. Christine recently reached out to me to better understand her Enneagram Eight husband and get some clarification on their relationship. One of the biggest struggles they seem to have is with communication. Christine always feels like Jeff is yelling, and Jeff says that he is not yelling at all and that is just how he speaks. When they have disagreements, Jeff will embrace them, whereas Christine will retreat and avoid the confrontation. That tends to cause Jeff to continue to push harder and Christine to retreat even more, which leads to an extreme breakdown in communication. Eights tend to be overcommunicators, and those who are in relationships with them need to learn how to balance their communication skills. Another way Christine learned to navigate her relationship with Jeff was by speaking up directly when he was doing or saying something that was hurtful. They also worked together to increase Jeff's ability to be vulnerable with emotions and feelings, which has helped their relationship significantly.

DATING AN ENNEAGRAM EIGHT

Enneagram Eights love to be in control, and it's the same way when going on dates with their partners. They usually like to know what is going on before they are placed into the situation. Not only that, but they typically prefer to plan the date themselves. This way they will know that they are doing exactly what they want to do. They are often only focused on feeling a connection with the other person and will make sure that their date is created around that. They also want to make sure that their date is focused on their partner and them being able to do whatever they want to do in that moment.

Relationships with Family

Enneagram Eights are very protective when it comes to their family. If you say something bad about or make fun of any of their family members, you will be sure to hear about it. They are the brother who always has your back, the parent who instills in their child to stand up for what they believe in, and the sister who will always give you her honest opinion. You never have to wonder what they are thinking or where you stand with them because they always tell you directly. They are often the leader of the family and sibling group, but they can be considered the aggressor if things don't go as planned. Some family members may feel like the Eight is being harsh with them if they don't understand that this is part of their personality. Remember what we said about friends? Eights feel like they are doing a disservice to their family members if they aren't completely honest with them, regardless of how it makes them feel. You will definitely be able to tell if a family member is an Eight because of their willingness to bend over backward to stick up for those who are important to them.

Brittany, a strong Enneagram Eight, has a pretty tight-knit family, consisting of two brothers and one sister, Anna. Anna is an Enneagram Two, The Helper. The dynamics between Brittany and Anna while they were growing up consisted of Brittany always sticking up for Anna, fighting her battles, and teaching her how to identify and use her voice. Anna always looked at Brittany as her protector, her heroine, her strong big sister. Obviously, there were some moments when they experienced issues, but it always came down to a breakdown of communication. Anna didn't love conflict, whereas Brittany thrived on it. Anna was pretty sensitive to Brittany's criticism, whereas Brittany felt like she was providing constructive criticism to ultimately help her. Anna was always quick to apologize, whereas Brittany felt that apologizing made her seem vulnerable or weak. It always comes down to being able to seek to understand those things about each other that leave you feeling confused. Once Anna knew those traits about Brittany, it strengthened their relationship and helped them know how to interact with each other better.

Be the Best Eight You Can Be

It's extremely hard for Eights to even want to sit down and read a chapter all about themselves because it forces them to be vulnerable and reveal their characteristics to others. But once Eights can learn how to be okay with vulnerability, that is when true growth can happen. We all have things we struggle with, but being open and honest about them will lead us to becoming the best versions of ourselves.

FIVE TIPS TO BE YOUR BEST
SELF IN THE REAL WORLD

1. Learn how to be patient with other people and recognize that not everyone is going to do things the way you do them.

2. Explore what it would look like to be okay with vulnerability. People want to see the real and raw you.

3. Recognize your anger, specifically what is making you feel angry. Learn to identify the root of the issue so you can keep it from becoming explosive.

4. Relinquish control sometimes. Taking the back seat at times will be helpful for growth because it will feel uncomfortable for you.

5. Try not to bottle up your emotions, because doing so will most likely lead to an explosive reaction later. If you feel a certain way about something, let it out in the moment.

PRACTICAL RELATIONSHIP STRATEGIES FOR A CHALLENGER

1. Surround yourself with like-minded people who will stand up for you and empower you when you need it.

2. Adjust your tone at times. Never lose your assertiveness but recognize who you're talking to and think about how they will receive what you are trying to say.

3. Remember that not everyone is trying to control you. Let those walls down. Let people in. People want to be in relationships with you.

4. Try to remember to express your appreciation and love for others. You might not need to hear it often, but they do.

5. Teach people how to stand up for themselves without always doing it for them. They will appreciate this in the long run.

Type

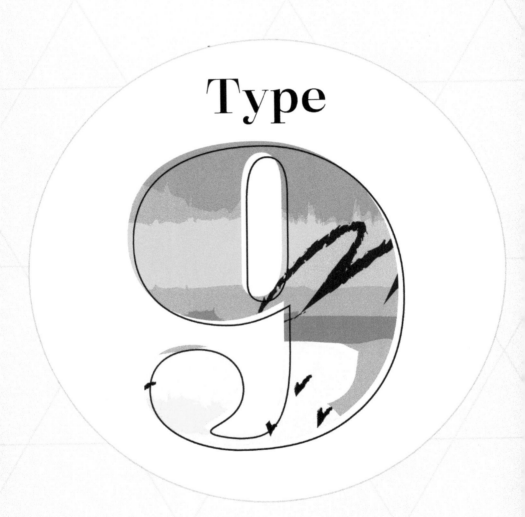

CHAPTER TEN

The Peacemaker

Everyone wants to be a Nine. If they don't want to be a Nine, then they want to be friends with Nines. For the most part, Nines have extremely good reputations because of their gentle souls, peacemaking tendencies, and ability to see multiple sides of a situation. Enneagram Nine, also known as *The Peacemaker,* has a desire to remain—you guessed it—peaceful. Specifically, Nines are motivated by a need to have inner stability and peace of mind. Their biggest fear is being separated or in conflict. With that being said, Nines absolutely despise conflict and will do whatever they have to do to avoid experiencing it. Let's dig deeper into what makes Nines one of the most desirable types.

Type **9**

Getting to Know The Peacemaker

When I think of Peacemakers, I always think of the people who are mediating conflict, keeping others calm in stressful situations, and just want everyone to get along. All of those things definitely describe typical qualities of a Nine. The word *peacemaker* is defined as "a person who brings about peace, especially by reconciling adversaries." Any time Nines experience conflict, it needs to be resolved immediately. Lingering conflict is literally their worst nightmare. When Nines are at their best, they are generous, patient, stable, and usually able to see the glass as half full. However, when they are at their worst, they can be passive-aggressive, unable to speak up, forgetful, and indecisive. Here are some other qualities of a Nine:

» Selfless

» Giving

» Open-minded

» Attentive

» Empathetic

» Advice-giving

» Calming

» Stubborn

» Unassertive

» Indifferent

» Peaceful

» Moderating

» Agreeable

» Welcoming

Common Mistypes

People can mistype as a Nine if they relate to hating conflict or being a people-pleaser. The reality is, a lot of people of all different types despise conflict and can relate to wanting to please people. Common mistypes as a Nine are Types Seven, Four, and Two. Nines and Sevens can seem similar at times because both types can be optimistic and try to avoid conflict because of the negativity it brings to their lives. However, some key differences are that Sevens are fast-paced and task-oriented, whereas Nines are slow starters and just want to enjoy the ride. Nines and Fours seem similar because they are both extremely empathetic, but Fours typically enjoy standing out, and Nines will always want to blend into a crowd. Nines and Twos are probably the most common mistype on the Enneagram. These two types can look extremely similar. For example, both tend to avoid conflict and enjoy pleasing others by giving of their time, effort, and skill set. The main way to determine if you're a Nine or a Two is to look at the motivations of the types. Are you a people-pleaser to avoid any conflict or negativity? Or are you a people-pleaser because you desire to be wanted? To figure out your type, always go back to the core motivation and fears of each one.

Childhood

Enneagram Nines in childhood are typically quiet and keep to themselves. They may feel ignored or like their opinions don't matter to their family members or siblings. Similar to adult Peacemakers, they tune out if there is any sort of conflict present. If the conflict is between other family members, they can often be seen trying to mediate the conflict. Even if they are mad at a sibling or family member, they won't say anything and will typically keep the anger bottled up inside. Somewhere along the way, they learned that their feelings are unimportant, and they live their childhood with bottled-up emotions and desires.

Worldview

Nines view the world as if it is full of strife and feel that they need to do something to remedy the conflict. By presenting a peaceful demeanor and assisting in mediation, they feel like they are doing their part to make the world a better place. Nines also view the world as if every person deserves to be respected and have a voice. By showing empathy and allowing others' opinions to be heard, they are fulfilling this worldview.

Strengths and Weaknesses

People generally love Nines because of their peaceful demeanors and their ability to always see both sides of a situation. They

Type

are the person you can go to if you need someone to play the devil's advocate, and Nines will always help you weigh the pros and cons of a scenario. They are extremely nonjudgmental and accept who you are wholeheartedly. Nines are also really good at being able to slow down and enjoy the little things in life. Relaxing is pretty much their middle name, and no one can do it quite like them. Like all types, Nines have weaknesses. They can be extremely indecisive because of their fear of creating conflict (within themselves) if they choose the wrong thing. They also tend to care a little too much about what others think of them, which often leaves them feeling bad about themselves. Another time they tend to feel bad about themselves is when they have an inability to get started. Nines are usually slow starters; the motivation is there, but they just can't begin. Like all Enneagram types, pursuing growth will allow for more of the positive traits to shine through.

Dealing with Conflict

Enneagram Nines are known for their desire to avoid conflict, so it probably comes as no surprise that is exactly what Nines do. Nines avoid conflict at all costs because it is physically and emotionally draining for them. However, sometimes Nines can act in a passive-aggressive way because of the bottled up feelings that they may have.

Enneagram Nine Wings

The wings of Enneagram Nine are very interesting because, to some, Nines and Eights might seem like total opposites. Though this can be true at times, a Nine with a strong Eight wing is a powerful combination. This type is more assertive than traditional Nines. Additionally, these Nines are better at displaying and acknowledging their opinions and ideas. Nines with a stronger access to the One wing are more structured than traditional Nines. They are more detail-oriented and generally more

THREE FAMOUS PEACEMAKERS

Enneagram Nines are harder to spot among famous people, probably because they tend to stay in the background. Three famous people who were Enneagram Nines are Walt Disney, Audrey Hepburn, and Mister Rogers.

- Walt Disney was the creator of Mickey Mouse and a pioneer in the entertainment and amusement park industries. He was a perfect example of a healthy Nine tapping into the positive qualities of a Three: motivated and driven with entrepreneurial tendencies.

- Similarly, Audrey Hepburn was a perfect example of a healthy Nine, with similar ambitious qualities. Extremely generous, almost to a fault, she was considered to be an incredibly charitable person.

- Fred Rogers, known as Mister Rogers, was the epitome of an Enneagram Nine. He brought peacefulness to the television screen starting in 1968. The show and Fred Rogers himself were known for values related to patience and "silence in a noisy world," as Maxwell King writes in his book about Mister Rogers's life. Mister Rogers did whatever he could to make this world a better and more peaceful place.

focused in general. By accessing both wings, Nines can grow into a healthier version of themselves.

Relationships with The Peacemaker

People love being in relationships with Peacemakers. I mean, come on, look at what they are called! And I'm talking any kind of relationships—friendships, family relationships, romantic relationships, working relationships, all of them. Peacemakers are usually extremely likeable people, so it's even annoying when our frenemies are Nines because you just can't dislike them. When I think of three words to describe relationships with The Peacemakers, they are supportive, passive, and comfortable.

Peacemakers are excellent at providing support to everyone with whom they are in relationships because of the amount of empathy they typically have. They can feel what people are going through and tend to carry that emotion along with them. Being nonjudgmental and offering support typically go hand in hand. You can always count on Enneagram Nines to be there for you when you need it, offer unbiased advice, and walk alongside you during the good times and the bad. No questions asked. No judgment received.

Peacemakers can also be passive, but that is simply to keep the peace and avoid conflict at all times. I'm not saying Nines don't have opinions or ideas (and amazing ones at that), it's just usually they go along with whatever the other person in the relationship wants because that's how they know they will be able to keep the peace. Nines are easygoing and pretty much the opposite of assertive. They want everyone around them to be okay and feel the same peace that they personally desire.

Finally, Nines thrive on comfort—on making themselves feel comfortable in relationships, yes, but also making sure that others feel just as comfortable. This could mean the environment they're in or simply physical comfort. They are also really good at relaxing and helping other people slow down and relax, which can be beneficial to people who are in relationships with them. Because they avoid conflict, they help make the situation more comfortable by mediating and offering unbiased advice.

Relationships with Colleagues

Peacemakers in work settings are exactly what they sound like: peacemakers. They typically keep to themselves and their own daily tasks and lie low so as not to draw attention to themselves. They do tend to have a difficult time starting tasks and often need the urging of a colleague to make sure that they complete them. Specific to relationships with their colleagues, Nines will always be there to offer a clear mind and unbiased opinion when you're trying to make or understand decisions. They are also much more willing to help you with your tasks than work on their own. When coworker drama occurs, Peacemakers will be nowhere to be found and would much rather not be involved. Peacemaker colleagues are kind, patient, and objective.

Tina (an Eight) and Joy (a Nine) have worked together on many projects at their marketing firm over the years. Tina knows she can rely on Joy's kindness and authenticity with their customers, but not necessarily the assertiveness to settle a contract. Tina has no problem taking the lead on this because she knows she has to. It's not that Joy doesn't want to, but it makes her uncomfortable to close the deal like that. Because Eights are natural leaders, this partnership works well because Tina can take the lead on most things, and Joy is a dependable colleague who enjoys some structure and direction. This again shows the beauty of the Enneagram—when people who are so different can get along well because they work to understand each other using this amazing tool.

Relationships with Friends

Friendships with Peacemakers can be absolutely amazing because of their ability and willingness to always be a listening ear and offer sound advice. However, it's important that you don't take advantage of this or they could withdraw from the friendship altogether. They want to make sure their voice is heard and that someone else is a listening ear for them. It can be hard for them to speak up when they want this, so as a friend, it's important that you learn these traits about your Nine. You might feel like you're always the one making decisions about what you're going to do on Friday night or where to go shopping, and you most likely will. But again, this doesn't mean they don't want to choose. They just don't want to rock the boat, so they will typically go along with whatever you want to do. Be mindful of this in your friendships with Nines, as they learn to navigate using their voice to demonstrate what they want and need.

Kayla (a Three) and Brian (a Nine) are fairly new friends who met at a social function last year. Kayla thinks Brian can be flaky at times. But to Brian, he's just removing himself from situations that could cause conflict. Brian feels like Kayla is too competitive and that nothing in life truly matters that much. But Kayla is more concerned with outward appearances than Brian is. Despite these differences, they get along well because Kayla can pull Brian out of his shell and reassure him that discussions can occur without conflict. Brian teaches Kayla that it's okay to relax and that sometimes it's necessary to be a healthy version of yourself. Kayla knows Brian is always there to weigh the pros and cons, be a listening ear, and offer advice.

Romantic Relationships

Peacemakers can make fantastic romantic partners because of their kind and welcoming personalities. Nines bring a large amount of comfort and support to their romantic partner and

DATING AN ENNEAGRAM NINE

This may not come as a surprise to you, but Enneagram Nines prefer to do whatever their partner wants to do. Because they are so accommodating to other people, it may be difficult for Nines to decide where they want to go or what they want to do for their date. Because of that, Enneagram Nines prefer to have the dates planned for them to take the pressure off of having to make decisions. Enneagram Nines will always prefer cozy dates and things that make them feel comfortable. Specific date ideas for Enneagram Nines include movie and pizza nights at home, trying out a new café, or having a picnic in a park.

definitely want to receive the same care in return. Nines are typically the calm, cool, and collected person in the relationship, and very little will rock their boat. Peacemakers hate conflict, even more so in romantic relationships. They want everything to remain peaceful between the two of you and will do whatever they can to resolve conflict situations immediately, or they will sweep things under the rug so they don't have to deal with it. Nines are great at listening and offering advice in a romantic relationship. Because of the comfort level usually associated with romantic relationships, Nines feel at home when they have someone in their corner to rely on, as well as being that person for someone else.

John (a Three) and Tom (a Nine) have been married for a few years. They have a lot of similarities and work well together because they are connected on the Enneagram. When John is stressed, he can take on some of the negative qualities of an Enneagram Nine. Similarly, when Tom is experiencing the healthy side of his personality type, he takes on the positive qualities of an Enneagram Three. However, John is extremely motivated all of the time. Driven by goals, he is always willing to take things to the next level. Tom is not that way at all and tends to need a gentle nudging from John to get started. This balance between the two works nicely as long as John is patient and understands when Tom just needs a little bit more time and guidance when making decisions.

Relationships with Family

Enneagram Nines in family structures usually keep everyone feeling happy and peaceful. They radiate a calm presence, and their family members genuinely enjoy being around them. They always avoid sibling conflict and tend to mediate it, as well as play devil's advocate while mediating. As parental figures, Peacemakers are supportive and assuring to their children. Because they aren't great at conflict, they will defer to their partner to discipline the children. They are usually the parent the child goes to because they won't say no. Overall, if you have an Enneagram Nine for a family member, consider yourself lucky and embrace the peaceful aura that surrounds them.

Shannon (a Four) is in college and her mom, Nancy, is an Enneagram Nine. Shannon talks to her mom frequently, despite being far away and busy with school. She knows she can rely on her mom for kindness and support regarding her friendship drama, but she also knows that she probably won't get the response she's looking for. When Shannon gives her mom the rundown of what has been happening in her friend group, her mom always wants her to view things from multiple perspectives. Shannon also says her mom just doesn't understand the drama and why it is happening. This is because Nines don't understand how anyone can get that worked up over a situation such as friend drama, which doesn't seem like a big deal to Nines. Shannon has learned that her mom will always make her consider multiple sides of the story and loves to go to her for advice, just not when she wants to be right.

Be the Best Nine You Can Be

Healthy Nines are some of the most amazing people in the world. They bring so much compassion, understanding, and peace to the world around them. Trying to be a healthy Nine is so much more than expressing your wants and desires and getting out of your comfort zone. Reflect on what you learned in this chapter and what you want to do with the information moving forward. Are you ready to take it to the next level?

FIVE TIPS TO BE YOUR BEST SELF IN THE REAL WORLD

1. When working to complete tasks, try to eliminate all distractions so you can focus on what is in front of you.

2. Practice the art of decision-making. Start with small decisions and work your way up to bigger ones. Make decisions based on your gut versus thinking it through entirely.

3. Practice expressing your emotions and specifically your anger. This will help prevent bottling them up and exploding later.

4. Instead of always being the advice-giver, learn how to ask for advice.

5. Practice time management to stay on track. Write things down and create a to-do list. Check things off and reward yourself for accomplishing them.

PRACTICAL RELATIONSHIP STRATEGIES FOR A PEACEMAKER

1. Don't sweep conflict and uncomfortable conversations under the rug. Force yourself to discuss it.

2. Communicate your wants and needs to your partner, and everyone else you are close to.

3. Try not to always go along with what the other person wants to do, eat, see, or explore. Be intentional about voicing your opinion and making sure your desires are met.

4. Try to get out of your comfort zone a little bit and rely on your partner to help you do that.

5. Identify when you're feeling angry and express it to your partner. Be open about your feelings and try not to be passive-aggressive toward others.

Richard Rohr

Eanneagram 4 Christian

CHAPTER ELEVEN

Where Do I Go from Here?

Now that you have an understanding of the Enneagram and how each of the types relate to one another, I'm sure you're wondering what exactly you're supposed to do with all this knowledge. Learning and understanding this information helps you better navigate your personal and professional relationships and understand how you see others, as well as how they view and interact with the world. Remember, the Enneagram tells us why we do the things that we do. You don't have all of the answers to why your coworker is silent in meetings or why your friend always wants you to go out once you have your pajamas on. But you might better understand the motivations behind these behaviors. It's also important to remember that you cannot assume anyone's Enneagram type—that is for them to figure out. If your partner, friend, or colleague doesn't know their type yet, don't pressure them. Give them space to discover it on their own. So, how do we put this information into practice?

The first thing to do is to be easy on yourself. What you just read about how you interact in relationships may not have felt very good. I'm sure there were some positive parts, but there were also negative things and maybe even concerning parts. That is totally okay, and honestly, that is the point of the Enneagram. You picked this book up for a reason. You wanted to better understand yourself, and now you are on your way to doing just that. So, breathe easy with this information, and use this book as a tool to recognize the traits you might not be happy about but also to remember that you're human and we are all just doing our best.

For Enneagram Ones, this may be hard for you, as it's difficult to silence your self-critic. But you can do it. I believe in you. Enneagram Two, being easy on yourself looks a lot like taking time to do things for yourself and not just for others. Enneagram Three, you don't always have to be the best at everything. Don't be so hard on yourself. Enneagram Four, try to remember that people love you for all of the things that make you unique. Enneagram Five, your knowledge is so needed in this world, but be gentle with yourself when you don't know everything. Enneagram Six, be kind to yourself when you're experiencing worry and anxiety. Identify the trigger, and learn how to counteract it. Enneagram Seven, be easy on yourself when you have to sit with negativity. I know you don't like it, but it's part of the growth process. Enneagram Eight, be patient on the road toward vulnerability. I know that it's difficult for you, but you are strong and capable of change. Enneagram Nine, be easy on yourself in the form of patience. I know conflict is hard for you, but be patient with the process.

The second thing to do is to be easy on *others*. Now that we know all of these things about how different types interact in relationships, we can understand some of the behaviors of others. We are not trying to excuse them, but we can seek to better understand those we love and are in relationships with on a daily basis. We can learn about and grow the relationships we have and think about ways to improve them. We can work toward better ways to communicate, ways to get along better with one another, and how to love one another not in the way that we want to receive love, but in a way that makes sense to who's receiving it.

Research, research, research. You don't have to be an Enneagram Five to love learning, especially when it comes to the Enneagram. You should not stop here. There are a ton of resources available for you to learn more about your type and how to relate to others. This should not be the end of the road for you and your knowledge. Take some time to reflect on the information you have learned, even if reflecting isn't your thing. See what resonates with you the most and which areas you need to work on. Maybe you need a trained Enneagram coach or expert to walk you through those areas, or maybe you feel like you can do it yourself. Either way, your Enneagram journey does not stop here. This is just the beginning.

Resources

Websites
EnneagramInstitute.com
TheEnneagramInBusiness.com
YourEnneagramCoach.com

Instagram
Beth McCord@yourenneagramcoach
Enneagram & Coffee@enneagramandcoffee
Enneagram Explained@enneagramexplained
Gina Gomez@ginagomez.co
Kristy Fountain@kristy.fountain
Steph Barron Hall@ninetypesco

Books
The Art of Typing: Powerful Tools for Enneagram Typing,
    by Ginger Lapid-Bogda
The Complete Enneagram: 27 Paths to Greater Self-Knowledge,
    by Beatrice Chestnut
The Enneagram Made Easy: Discover the 9 Types of People,
    by Renee Baron and Elizabeth Wagele
*Millenneagram: The Enneagram Guide for Discovering Your
    Truest, Baddest Self,* by Hannah Paasch
*The Path Between Us: An Enneagram Journey to Healthy
    Relationships,* by Suzanne Stabile
*The Road Back to You: An Enneagram Journey to
    Self-Discovery,* by Ian Morgan Cron and Suzanne Stabile
*The Wisdom of the Enneagram: The Complete Guide to Psycho-
    logical and Spiritual Growth for the Nine Personality Types,*
    by Don Richard Riso and Russ Hudson

References

Cron, Ian Morgan and Suzanne Stabile. *The Road Back to You: An Enneagam Journey to Self-Discovery.* Downer's Grove, IL: InterVarsity Press, 2016.

King, Maxwell. *The Good Neighbor: The Life and Work of Fred Rogers.* New York, NY: Abrams Press, 2018.

Lapid-Bogda, Ginger. *The Art of Typing: Powerful Tools for Enneagram Typing.* Santa Monica, CA: The Enneagram in Business Press, 2018.

Index

Acknowledgments

I've hesitated to write my acknowledgments because of serious fear that I'm going to forget someone. If that doesn't scream "Enneagram Two," I don't know what will. There were so many people who contributed to the success of the book, likely without even knowing they were doing so.

First of all, I have to thank Callisto Publishing for believing in my ability to produce this book. Specifically, Joe Cho and Emily Angell, my incredible editor. Emily, you were so patient and understanding with me as a first-time author and you gave me the confidence to continue to move forward. You were the first person to make me believe that I was an actual author. To the artistic team, you literally brought my dreams and my vision of this book to life. As a visual person, I couldn't imagine what my first book would look like. Then I saw it and I cried and cried and cried. Callisto Publishing, you have made my dreams come true and I am eternally grateful.

To my Instagram community, you all show up daily wanting to put in the work to better understand yourself and others using the framework of the Enneagram. You all inspire me to keep creating content and to keep being my authentic self.

To my friends who I have neglected over the past several months because of the busyness of writing a book, thank you for still loving me. Molly, thank you for reading my writing sample for this book and telling me that I can do this. Whitney, thank you for constantly reminding me how excited you are to read this book. Lisa, Tiff, and Melissa, you all inspired me to show my personality more on my platform and you all remind me daily how proud you are of me. I'm even more proud of all of you. Lindsey and Sarah, thank you for your constant encouragement and reminding me that I'm a badass. Christine, thank you for your endless support and encouragement when I chase my crazy dreams.

To Donna and Curt Ober, I feel so blessed to have you as my in-laws. I don't know how I got so lucky. Thank you for letting me love your son, and supporting me unconditionally.

To my family: Mom and Whit, you have always supported every move that I have made. You have shown me what I can accomplish in life. You have loved me into who I am today. Dad and Cindy, I can feel your pride from here. Thank you for being an example of what hard work looks like and for your endless support. To my siblings, Steve, Amanda, Nick, Becky, and Matt, we've come a long way from your blank stares while I talked about the Enneagram. I love each of you so much, and I have so appreciated the encouragement throughout this process. Remember when Nick made you all go around the table and say what you loved about me? All of your words coated this Enneagram Two heart with everything I needed to move forward. And to my sister, Britt, my Enneagram Eight protector. My heroine. You've always had my back and my front. You have paved the way for me to stand on my own two feet. Thank you for reminding me to know my value and to fight for what I deserve. You're the best and I love co-hosting the Say Enneathing podcast with you (shameless plug).

Finally, my husband. Derek, you are so much more than a husband to me. You're my best friend. My partner. My equal. The best encourager and cheerleader there ever was. There have been multiple times where I panicked and thought I couldn't do this. You were always there to remind me I could do anything I put my mind to. I couldn't have done this without you. I love you.

About the Author

Ashton Whitmoyer-Ober, MA is a community psychologist and certified Enneagram coach. She received her BA in psychology from East Carolina University and her MA in community psychology and social change from Pennsylvania State University. An entrepreneur at heart, she opened her own business at 22. She was featured in Mika Brzezinski's book *Know Your Value*, involved in the MSNBC Grow Your Value contest, and her writing has been published on MSNBC.com. Since closing her retail business, Glitz Boutique, Ashton works in the sexual and relationship violence prevention field and has her own Enneagram and life coaching business, Enneagram Ashton. Ashton is a writer, public speaker, and advocate for the underdog. She lives in central Pennsylvania with her husband and rescue puppy. This is her first book. You can find her on Instagram at @enneagramashton.